KATE MULVANY OAM is an award-winning playwright, screenwriter and actor. Her epic adaptation of the Ruth Park trilogy *The Harp in the South* played to great acclaim for the Sydney Theatre Company in 2018, and she followed this with her adaptation of Schiller's *Mary Stuart* for the company in 2019. Her play *The Rasputin Affair* was produced at the Ensemble Theatre and her play *Jasper Jones*, an adaptation of Craig Silvey's novel, has enjoyed great success at Belvoir Street Theatre, MTC, QTC and State Theatre Company of South Australia after its Barking Gecko premiere in 2015. In 2015 Mulvany's play *Masquerade*, a reimagining of the much-loved children's book by Kit Williams, was performed at the 2015 Sydney Festival and the State Theatre Company of South Australia as well as Melbourne Festival, produced by Griffin Theatre Company. Her autobiographical play *The Seed* (Belvoir Street Theatre) won the Sydney Theatre Award for Best Independent Production. With Mulvany performing in the play, it received great critical success and toured nationally, and is currently being developed into a work for screen. Mulvany's *Medea*, co-written with Anne-Louise Sarks, having been produced by Belvoir Street Theatre in 2012, won several awards including an AWGIE Award and five Sydney Theatre Awards, and has gone on to be produced in Poland, Basel, Auckland and at the Gate Theatre in London, to rave reviews. Other plays and musicals include *The Mares* for the Tasmanian Theatre Company, *The Danger Age*, *Blood and Bone*, *The Web*, the musical *Somewhere* (music by Tim Minchin) and *Storytime*, which won Mulvany the 2004 Philip Parsons Award. As a screenwriter, she has worked on several television series, including *Beat Bugs* (the Emmy-award-winning series for Netflix) and the critically acclaimed *Upright* for Lingo Pictures. She is also an award-winning stage and screen actor with credits with many Australian theatre companies, television series and films. Most recently she played the eponymous role in *Richard III* (Bell Shakespeare) to great critical and popular acclaim, the one-person play *Every Brilliant Thing* (Belvoir Theatre) and can be seen as Sister Harriet in the acclaimed Amazon Prime series *Hunters*.

Lena Cruz (left) and Catherine Văn-Davies in Sydney Theatre Company's 2021 production of Playing Beatie Bow. *(Photo: Daniel Boud)*

PLAYING BEATIE BOW

ADAPTED BY
Kate Mulvany

FROM THE NOVEL BY
Ruth Park

CURRENCY PRESS
The performing arts publisher

CURRENCY PLAYS

First published in 2021
by Currency Press Pty Ltd,
PO Box 2287, Strawberry Hills, NSW, 2012, Australia
enquiries@currency.com.au
www.currency.com.au

Copyright: *Conversations across time: the joyous stage production of* Playing Beatie Bow © Vanessa Berry, 2021; *Playing Beatie Bow* © Kate Mulvany and Kemalde Pty Ltd, 2021.

COPYING FOR EDUCATIONAL PURPOSES

The Australian *Copyright Act 1968* (Act) allows a maximum of one chapter or 10% of this book, whichever is the greater, to be copied by any educational institution for its educational purposes provided that that educational institution (or the body that administers it) has given a remuneration notice to Copyright Agency (CA) under the Act.
For details of the CA licence for educational institutions contact CA, 11/66 Goulburn Street, Sydney, NSW, 2000; tel: within Australia 1800 066 844 toll free; outside Australia 61 2 9394 7600; fax: 61 2 9394 7601; email: info@copyright.com.au

COPYING FOR OTHER PURPOSES

Except as permitted under the Act, for example a fair dealing for the purposes of study, research, criticism or review, no part of this book may be reproduced, stored in a retrieval system, or transmitted in any form or by any means without prior written permission. All enquiries should be made to the publisher at the address above.

Any performance or public reading of *Playing Beatie Bow* is forbidden unless a licence has been received from the author or the author's agent. The purchase of this book in no way gives the purchaser the right to perform the play in public, whether by means of a staged production or a reading. All applications for public performance should be addressed to Cameron's Management, Locked Bag 848, Surry Hills 2010; ph: +61 2 9319 7199; info@cameronsmanagement.com.au

The introduction on page vii was originally published in *The Conversation* and is reproduced under a Creative Commons licence.
Typeset by Dean Nottle for Currency Press.
Cover design by Emma Bennetts.
Currency Press acknowledges the Traditional Owners of the Country on which we live and work. We pay our respects to all Aboriginal and Torres Strait Islander Elders, past and present.

A catalogue record for this book is available from the National Library of Australia

Contents

Conversations across time: the joyous stage production of Playing Beatie Bow   *vii*

Author's note   *xi*

Playing Beatie Bow

     Act One   1

     Act Two   50

References   98

Dedication:

*For Tara Neilsen
'Honour bright'.*

Conversations across time: the joyous stage production of *Playing Beatie Bow*

Playing Beatie Bow is the coming-of-age story of the teenage Abigail who, from her home in Sydney's The Rocks, slips back in time to 1873. Here, she is taken in by the Tallisker/Bow family, immigrants from the Orkney Islands who run a confectionery shop. Abigail finds herself cast as the mysterious 'Stranger'—the subject of a Tallisker family prophecy—which she must enact before she is able to return to her own time.

In adapting Ruth Park's novel for the stage, Kate Mulvany carries forward Park's detailed, loving attention to the city of Sydney and the lives that play out within it. Her adaptation thrums with heart, humour and a sense of creative legacy.

Ruth Park's long and distinguished literary career began at the *Auckland Star* in the 1930s. In 1942, she moved to Sydney, the city which she would go on to capture with such verve and particularity. By the time of her death in 2010, aged 93, she was one of Australia's most loved and successful authors.

Park's skill in writing for young adults was to portray the emotional intensity of adolescence alongside a broader sweep of time and history, and this production takes place in almost the very location in which the story is set. The qualities of The Rocks which so captivated Park—the steep topography, the narrow terrace houses, the crooked laneways—still produce a sense of a lingering past.

Many in the audience would have travelled through these streets to arrive at the theatre. There is a clear delight in this proximity, and the opening scenes set in the present day further develop this rapport, referencing the pandemic, distractions of social media, and that inevitable Sydney topic: the excesses of the city's real estate.

Names and objects are powerful in *Playing Beatie Bow*. In Park's research for the novel she compiled long lists of potential Victorian-era names, deliberating over which would best carry the distinctions of her characters. Park was rigorous in her historical research, with a particular interest in seeking out the everyday details of 19th-century working-class life in Sydney. The heavy 19th-century garments, chamber pots, ceramic 'hot-pig' water bottle and the glass jars of boiled lollies work to as veritable effect on stage as they do in the novel. These details are highlighted in David Fleischer's spare, dynamic set design.

Mulvany's inclusion of Aboriginal characters, language and recognition of country is a striking addition to Park's original story. In the present day, Abigail (Catherine Văn-Davies) visits her Gadigal neighbours, greets them *'worimi'*, and knows The Rocks equally as Tallawoladah. In the 19th century, Abigail continues this connection with the Tallisker's neighbour with whom she strikes up a friendship. Mulvany converts Park's characters of the Chinese laundrymen to Johnny Whites (Guy Simon), an Aboriginal laundryman. Through Whites the trauma and fracture of colonial dispossession for Aboriginal land and people is given voice.

As Abigail's slip in time provides opportunities for reflection on social changes and injustices, it also brings humour. As Abigail and Beatie (Sofia Nolan) compare observations of each others' times, Beatie expresses bemusement over the 'palm-books' everyone in the future is looking down at and examining with such intensity. What book must it be, Beatie muses, maybe the Gospels? This is Mulvany, but so absolutely in line with Park's sensibilities I imagined her laughing along with the audience.

The cast revel in their portrayal of these time disjunctions, and in delivering the Tallisker's Scots vocabulary. Mulvany takes one term in particular, *spaewife*, as a letimotif in the production. In Scots, a *spaewife* is a fortune-teller; a woman possessing a magic enabling communication across time. The Talliskers call it The Gift and it is carried by Granny (Heather Mitchell), the family's matriarch.

Repeated in speech and song throughout the play, this word takes on a symbolic presence. In a story so much about legacy—particularly the connections and lineages that connect women—*spaewife* becomes broadly symbolic of women's power. This power radiates through the play, in the connections between characters and generations, and in between Park and Mulvany as writers. There is no better embodiment of this power than in Beatie, played with an electric intensity by Nolan. Her force as a character is her quick tongue and determination to live a life greater than what is prescribed for women of her time.

The character of Beatie Bow was inspired by a girl in an 1899 street photograph from The Rocks, which Park came across in the 1940s. She describes the scene in her autobiography, *Fishing in the Styx* (1993): how she returned again and again to look at this 'sharp-faced' girl who carried a defiant expression. The girl seemed to be speaking to her through time, challenging her not to take her for less than she is.

Thirty years later, Park wrote *Playing Beatie Bow*. Now, forty years on again, through Mulvany's fierce and fond version for the stage, Beatie's voice speaks to us with a renewed energy.

Vanessa Berry

This article first appeared in *The Conversation* in March 2021 as a review to the Sydney Theatre Company production titled 'Playing Beatie Bow is brought to thundering life in a joyous stage production'. Vanessa Berry is a writer of literary nonfiction with a focus on place-writing and memoir. Her works include *Mirror Sydney*, *Ninety9*, *Strawberry Hills Forever* and *I am a Camera*. Her collection of essays, *Gentle and Fierce*, will be published by Giramondo in 2021.

This adaptation was written on Gadigal Land.

The playwright honours and respects the Traditional Owners and Storytellers of this land – past, present and future.

Always was, always will be Aboriginal land.

Author's note

Ruth Park drops breadcrumbs. As you walk along the pathways of her vast and varied work, it's easy to be dazzled by the big ideas—the imaginative leaps, the feminist insights, the swathes of history, the epic love stories, the diverse and ever-shifting communities. But look closer at that pathway, and you'll see it's also speckled with delicious morsels of information that season the narrative even further. Seemingly throwaway references to 'Infant Phenomenons' and disease-addled ships named 'Corona', ostrich-plumed 'high-steppers' and 'grass of Parnassus'—all of these are mentioned only once or twice in *Playing Beatie Bow*, but they cannot be ignored. When you shine a light on them, they become jewels in a treasure chest of time—with every gem polished and placed by Ruth Park herself. She watches from afar, waiting to see if you'll notice them glinting.

One of these 'breadcrumbs', for me, popped up out of nowhere on page 101 of my dog-eared copy of *Playing Beatie Bow*, on about my third read in preparation for this adaptation. It is the word *'spaewife'* and it is only mentioned one other time after that in the book. 'There ne'er was such a spaewife as Granny in her young days,' says Dovey about her grandmother Alice Tallisker. I was intrigued by this word, and Ruth's use of it—tucked away quietly amidst the rollicking Rocks story. I picked up the word and dived into its etymology. *'Spae'* is a Nordic-Scots word that means 'to foretell'—a word filled with unknown context. And yet 'wife' ... What does 'wife' mean here? What was Ruth trying to tell us by using it? After having the weary matriarch Margaret Darcy scream from the pages of *The Harp in the South* 'WHAT'S A BODY BORN FOR?!', suddenly this surprising use of the word 'wife' had taken on a new quality between Ruth's books. It wasn't attached to being married to a man or the mother of offspring, like in the *Harp* trilogy. Instead, it seemed to have a uniquely different femme power, and when I looked closer, all of her characters—no matter how they identified—seemed to have this power within them, whether they knew it or not. The power to listen and learn from the lessons whispered on the wind.

You see, Ruth herself was a spaewife. Time and again, her novels have seen into the future, dissected the present and reached into the past with startling accuracy and brutal honesty. And as someone who told the stories of ordinary, working-class communities of diverse individuals, she made sure she never withheld the magic from these people. Instead, they were the keepers of it. She saw the power in their sharing of stories, spells, songs, legends, legacy and culture and she spun a magic throughout her tales that to this day makes for a bewitching journey as a reader. It also makes her work an absolute gift to bring to the stage and to audiences of all ages.

Ruth's characters and communities are grimed with hard-worn history. But they also come with a purpose. After the last page is read and the book is closed, her characters still whisper to us, 'Will you remember me? Will you pass on my story? Did you pick up the breadcrumbs we dropped? What do our stories mean to you? How will you walk out of our world and into your own? And what story will you leave etched into the rocks of your time?'

To know that stories have been shared for over 60,000 years on the land we are gathered on is awe-inspiring and humbling. To open the new Wharf Theatre in a space that Ruth's stories and characters actually came from is amazing. And to have artists and audiences become a community in any theatre, if only for a blink of time, is one of the most magical of gifts we have now, in our past, and—I hope—the infinite future.

We can all be spaewives. We all have within us the power to honour the ancient stories of the land we walk on, celebrate the people from all walks of life and time that we walk amongst, and ensure those stories and songs are listened to, heeded and take us toward a better future together.

I thank the stars for Ruth Park, and I'm so grateful to Rory Niland, Tim Curnow and the Park Estate for trusting me once again with her magnificent words and worlds. Thanks to my English teacher Ms Hammond who first put *Playing Beatie Bow* in my hands when I was twelve years old and made me a Ruth Park fan for life. Thank you to Kip Williams, Polly Rowe and all at the Sydney Theatre Company for your ongoing support of Australian artists and stories. Thank you to Courtney Stewart, my incredible dramaturg and sounding board.

AUTHOR'S NOTE

Thank you to the astounding team of cast and creatives who shared their own stories and legacies and always bring such pride and passion to their work as artists—one of the most ancient (and important) jobs in the world. Thank you to Anne Crawley and all at The Rocks Walking Tours for letting this playwright tag along and harangue them with never-ending questions. Thanks to Matt Webb and the Sydney Festival for the incredible Burrawa tour that showed me an ancient Sydney that should be taught to us all. Thanks to Matthew Doyle for sharing his beautiful Gadigal songs, language and consultation and Phuong Văn for her gorgeous lullaby. Thanks to Sam Hagan and Maggie Patton at the State Library of NSW for the maps of Sydney/Tallowoladah. Thank you to my partner Hamish Michael for putting up with me jabbering and singing in a multitude of accents over the past year of writing this play from Covid lockdown. Finally, thank you to the First Nations people of this country—the original and eternal story-sharers of this land. Always was, always will be Aboriginal land.

I hope you enjoy this walk through time down the pathway of past, present and future. Make sure you pick up the breadcrumbs …

Kate Mulvany
January 2021

Sofia Nolan (left) and Catherine Văn-Davies in Sydney Company's 2021 production of PLAYING BEATIE BOW. (Photo: Daniel Boud)

Playing Beatie Bow was first produced by Sydney Theatre Company at The Wharf 1 Theatre, Sydney, on 26 February 2021, with the following cast:

WEYLAND / MR BOW / CAST	Tony Cogin
KATHY / CAST	Lena Cruz
DOVEY / CAST	Claire Lovering
MARGARET / GRANNY	Heather Mitchell
BEATIE BOW	Sofia Nolan
JUDAH / JONAH / CAST	Rory O'Keeffe
JOHNNY WHITES / CAST	Guy Simon
ABIGAIL KIRK / CAST	Catherine Văn-Davies
GIBBIE / VINNIE / CAST	Ryan Yeates

Director, Kip Williams
Set Designer, David Fleischer
Costume Designer, Renée Mulder
Lighting Designer, Nick Schlieper
Composer, Clemence Williams
Sound Designer, David Bergman
Choral Director, Natalie Gooneratne
Additional Composition, Matthew Doyle
Dramaturg, Courtney Stewart
Assistant Director, Kenneth Moraleda
Fight, Movement and Intimacy Director, Nigel Poulton
Voice and Text Coach, Danielle Roffe
Production Manager, Genevieve Jones
Stage Manager, Minka Stevens
Deputy Stage Manager, Katie Hankin
Assistant Stage Manager, Brooke Kiss

CHARACTERS

BEATIE BOW, 11, white
ABIGAIL KIRK, 16, Vietnamese-Australian
KATHY, 42, Vietnamese-Australian
MARGARET, 67, white
JUSTIN, 35, First Nations Australian
TREVOR, 45, white
VINNIE, 10, white
DYLAN, 16, white
MEL, 16, white
WEYLAND, 45, white
MR BOW, 45, white
GRANNY, 70, white
DOVEY, 21, white
JUDAH, 18, white
GIBBIE, 10, white
JOHNNY WHITES, 30s, First Nations Australian
PUSHER 1, 2, 3, 4, 5
SPAEWIFE (shared role)
ERNEST
HANNAH
MAUDE
DOLLY
JONAH, 19, white
LOCALS OF THE ROCKS

Playwright's note:

The above casting descriptions represent the original cast of *Playing Beatie Bow*. The playwright asks that all productions be inclusive and diverse in their casting.

SUGGESTED CHARACTER DOUBLINGS

BEATIE BOW
ABIGAIL KIRK / SPAEWIFE
KATHY / DOLLY / SPAEWIFE
MARGARET / GRANNY
DOVEY / MEL / MAUDE / PUSHER 2
JUSTIN / JOHNNY WHITES / PUSHER 1 / ERNEST
VINNIE / GIBBIE / PUSHER 3
WEYLAND / MR BOW / HANNAH
TREVOR / DYLAN / JUDAH / JONAH
LOCALS OF THE ROCKS – whoever is available!

SETTING

The Rocks, Sydney.
2021 and 1873.

TEXT NOTE

Text in **regular bold** font indicates sung lyrics.

Text in ***bold italic*** font indicates descriptive text quoted directly as it appears in Ruth Park's original book.

Cast of Sydney Theatre Company's 2021 production of Playing Beatie Bow. *(Photo: Daniel Boud)*

ACT ONE

SCENE ONE

In darkness, children's voices float through space and time, singing an ancient, eerie rhyme.

CHILDREN'S VOICES: **Oh, Mudda, what's that? What's that?**
CHILD: **Nothing at all … The dog at the door …**

A teenage girl—ABIGAIL KIRK—*sits alone by a lamppost.*

VOICES: **Oh, Mudda, what's that? What's that?**
CHILD: **The wind in the chimney, that's all, that's all.**
VOICES: **Oh, Mudda, what's that? Can you see?**
CHILD: **The cow in the byre … The horse in the stall …**

Slowly, slowly … a figure appears onstage, emerging from the darkness. She is BEATIE BOW.

'Her face was pale and her hair was clipped so close it looked like cat's fur. She wore a long, washed-out print dress, a pinafore of brown cotton, and a shawl crossed over her chest.'

VOICES: **Oh, Mudda, what's that in the shadows?**
CHILD: **A fox in its hole … A hare in its burrow …**
VOICES: **Oh, Mudda, I see something there!**
CHILD: **Close your eyes, bairn, shhh shhh, there there …**

BEATIE *walks toward* ABIGAIL, *her arms lifting as she approaches, reaching out for the girl.*

VOICES: **Oh, Mudda, what's that up ahead?!**
CHILD: **It's Beatie Bow! Back from the *dead!***

The children scream. And BEATIE BOW *disappears into thin air.*

SCENE TWO

An apartment, high above Sydney, 2021. ABIGAIL *and her mother* KATHY *are going through an old trunk of antique bits and bobs. Kathy's mother-in-law* MARGARET *peers out of a window.*

'Abigail was thin and flat as a board, with a narrow brown face and black coffee eyes. Long brown hair and black, straight eyebrows.' She wears a long vintage green dress and boots and sits quietly, assisting her mother.

KATHY wears overalls, with her hair *'raked up on top of her head in a washerwoman's knot.'* She hums an ancient tune softly as she sorts through the trunk.

MARGARET—*Abigail's grandmother—takes in the view as she sips from a cup of tea.*

'She was chic and glittery and poisonous.'

MARGARET: Good Lord, I could never live this high—if there was a fire you'd have no hope. How many more climbers can they cram onto the Bridge, do you think? There's five lots up there already—only a matter of time before the whole thing collapses. So much construction, more cranes than buildings—the giraffes at Taronga will think it's bloody mating season. Very kind of Weyland's firm to let you live here—I mean, what's it worth, Katherine? Five, five point five? Of course, we were never allowed to venture into this area when I was young. Slums. You can feel it, can't you? It's etched into The Rocks. Still, at least it's central, I suppose.

Beat.

What is that God-awful thing, Katherine?

KATHY: It's an old bridal chest. So much inside—my clients will love it.

MARGARET: Where on earth did you find it?

KATHY: The council flats around the corner. Deceased estate. Just turfed out on the cobblestones with 'Please Take Me' scrawled on a note.

MARGARET: It smells putrid.

KATHY: I don't smell anything.

MARGARET: Because you're used to it, dear. Desensitised.

KATHY: There's bound to be some treasure we can sell at Magpies if we keep digging, right, Abigail?

ABIGAIL *gives a small smile and nods.*

MARGARET: Along with plenty of vermin, no doubt.

KATHY: I had to deal with plenty more vermin as a lawyer, Margaret.

The worst kind. The ones with red ties and chardonnay breath. Now, Abigail, let's put all this in order.

> KATHY *holds up items as examples, starting with a portrait of Queen Victoria.*

Victorian. Edwardian. Art Deco. New Age. COVID.

> MARGARET *hurriedly puts on her COVID mask.* KATHY *continues to pull items from the trunk.*

MARGARET: How's the new school, Lynette?

ABIGAIL: [*softly*] My name is Abigail.

> MARGARET *rolls her eyes.*

MARGARET: *Abigail.* What classes are you taking?

ABIGAIL: English Extension 2, Earth and Environmental Science, Extension 2 Maths, Physics and Drama.

MARGARET: Oh, Drama doesn't count though, does it, not in the real world. Have you made any little friends? Who do you sit with?

ABIGAIL: No-one.

MARGARET: Ah. Social distancing.

ABIGAIL: No, Granny. I just don't want to.

MARGARET: Oh. You know the other children might be nicer to you if you weren't so weird, Lynette.

KATHY: Margaret—

MARGARET: Sorry—*Abigail.* Sixteen-year-olds don't dress like that. They wear jeans and trainers and lip gloss and ear bugs. They don't traipse about looking like some forlorn lice-ridden bread thief headed straight for Botany bloody Bay. I mean, what era is that trip hazard from?

KATHY: I think that dress is from a time all of its own. It's fabulously unique.

MARGARET: It's straight out of a bloody theatre restaurant. And as for this name change—I don't know what's wrong with her real name. Lynette is a very pretty name.

KATHY: She just prefers Abigail.

MARGARET: Abigail is a witch's name. A heathen little troublemaking harlot at that.

KATHY: I like Abigail. It's a good, strong name.

MARGARET: Well, regardless of what she calls herself, she'll never get a boyfriend looking like that.

KATHY: She may not want a boyfriend.

MARGARET: Well, she'll never get a girlfriend either. See? I'm very open-minded, Katherine. I'm very woke. I marched for women, you know, Abigail, with your father in my arms—right the way up Macquarie Street.

ABIGAIL: Maybe you should've left him there.

> ABIGAIL *has found something in the bridal chest—***'a strangely shaped piece of yellowed crochet.'**

What's this, Mum?

> KATHY *inspects it.*

KATHY: It's some kind of lace. Embroidered with … I think it's … grass of Parnassus.

ABIGAIL: Grass of Parnassus …

KATHY: Parnassus is a faraway land where the goddesses of poetry and music and art, dance and sing and share their stories.

> MARGARET *laughs suddenly. She holds out her phone.*

MARGARET: Look at this puppy on a pig.

> *But* ABIGAIL *is transfixed on the crochet.*

ABIGAIL: Between the leaves of every flower … Are they initials? A? T?

KATHY: It's so discoloured, I can't make it out …

ABIGAIL: It's so beautiful. It's exactly what I've been looking for, this dress. Don't you think? Around the collar? Can I have it, Mum?

KATHY: If you can bring it back from the dead, sure.

ABIGAIL: Can you soak it for me? I'm going next door—I promised Justin I'd take Vinnie to the park this afternoon.

> *She goes to leave.*

KATHY: Oh, Abigail … I'm catching up with a friend tonight.

ABIGAIL: Again? Oh.

KATHY: Will you be alright at home by yourself?

ABIGAIL: Yep.

> *She goes to leave.*

ACT ONE

KATHY: My little witch … *Mẹ yêu con.*

ABIGAIL turns and gives a reluctant smile.

ABIGAIL: Love you too, Mum.

She gives KATHY *a kiss.*

MARGARET: Lynette …

She rolls her eyes.

Abigail.

She gestures to ABIGAIL. ABIGAIL *hesitates then walks toward* MARGARET.

No matter what happened between my son and your mother, you and I are still connected. I will always be your …

She can't say it.

ABIGAIL: Grandmother.

MARGARET *nods and offers a sanitary elbow to* ABIGAIL. *She ignores it.*

You know where we got that teacup, Gran? In the last trunk Mum found on the street.

MARGARET *almost gags as she puts the teacup aside. As* ABIGAIL *walks away, she trips over the dress slightly but forges on.*

MARGARET: That girl is utterly peculiar.

KATHY: She's sixteen, Margaret. She's still growing into herself.

MARGARET: She's a shifty little shrew. Hardly says a word to anyone but is perfectly happy to rob you blind at the slightest chance she gets. You should have come down harder with that shoplifting nonsense, Katherine. From a St Vinnies of all things! Shameful.

KATHY: It was just an old petticoat. She wanted to wear it under that dress.

MARGARET: Well, it must come from your side. Her father never did anything of the sort. Does she see much of him? Weyland?

KATHY: She needs more time.

MARGARET: Do you see much of him? Since the divorce came through?

KATHY: He's your son, Margaret. Ask him yourself.

MARGARET: He's not answering my FaceTimes. Is he still seeing that woman?

KATHY: *Margaret!*

KATHY keeps sorting.

That's all in the past now. Everything that's coming is good. I can hear the wind singing to me and Abby as it whips through The Rocks ... Listen. Do you hear?

As MARGARET *tries to hear,* KATHY *hums her tune and continues going through the bridal chest.* MARGARET *rolls her eyes and peers back out the window. Her diatribe starts again ...*

MARGARET: Good Lord, the Opera House needs a scrub—it's looking positively jaundiced. Utzon would be rolling in his grave. Again.

Beat. She sips.

Where's my watch?

SCENE THREE

The sound of a television screen screeching a hideous electronic children's tune.

We see a flat not dissimilar to Abigail and Kathy's, only a little more dilapidated.

JUSTIN CROWN *is on the phone as he wades through a mess of laundry, toys and textbooks.*

JUSTIN: [*on the phone*] I've put the lotion on him three times, Francine, and not the natural organic stuff either—the hardcore napalm for the scalp. I mean, even a cockroach couldn't outlive this potion, and I've put it on my kid's head three times this week. Have you ever thought it could be those Campbell twins, Francine? The ginger ones with the hair down to their bums who aren't vaccinated? I know if I was a nit, that's where I'd bunker down. No chance of execution in those follicles. I'm telling you, Francine, the head lice didn't come from Vinnie, he's clean as a—

A man in high-vis FIFO work gear—TREVOR—*hurries through. He kisses* JUSTIN *and gestures a goodbye to a figure on the couch.*

[*To* TREVOR] Love you.

ACT ONE

TREVOR: Love you. Gotta go.
JUSTIN: *Yanu.* Stay safe.

ABIGAIL appears at their apartment.

TREVOR: *Yanu.* Can't stop, Abby. Airport traffic.
ABIGAIL: 'Bye, Trevor. *Warami*, Justin.

JUSTIN smiles in relief at ABIGAIL *and hands her a backpack. He gestures a signal to a young boy on the couch whose eyes never leave the telly—* VINNIE.

JUSTIN: [*to* VINNIE] Abby's here, Vinnie. Say *warami*.
VINNIE: *Warami*, Abby.
JUSTIN: It speaks! Praise be! [*Back to the phone*] Oh, rest assured, Francine, I will have a chat to my husband about it, but when he's home on FIFO the last thing he wants to do is talk about 'obligate ectoparasites' and the first thing he wants to do is not appropriate for me to talk to a student teacher about. Alright then? Hoo-roo.

He hangs up.

You're a lifesaver, Abby. The primary school's been infested with head lice again, Trev's been called back to the trenches, I've got a social work paper due tomorrow and all I've done is chosen the font for the title page. Antiqua Italic. Underlined. What do you reckon?
ABIGAIL: Very refined.
JUSTIN: Take your hoodie, Vinnie. Windy out there today, mate.

He fishes one out of the detritus.

And here's a twenty, Abby. Please take it. You know how much babysitters charge these days?
VINNIE: I'm not a baby.

ABIGAIL takes the money and puts it in her dress pocket.

JUSTIN: Nice watch. That new?
ABIGAIL: Inherited from my gran.
JUSTIN: Ah. How's school going? Settled in yet?
ABIGAIL: Not much point. Only gonna be there a year and then I'll be moving as far away from here as I can.
JUSTIN: Still not a fan of The Rocks?
ABIGAIL: Nothing to do except dodge tour groups or spend a fortune on kangaroo scrotums made into coin purses. Everyone's so busy taking

pictures of themselves with a fake convict they don't see who actually lives here. May as well not exist at all.

JUSTIN: There's more to Tallowolodah than meets the eye. You'll see.

ABIGAIL: I've seen enough.

VINNIE: Are we going to see the furry girl, Abby?

ABIGAIL: Furry girl?

VINNIE: She's a ghost. From the past. And she rises from her grave and everyone runs and pretends to be afraid. But the furry girl doesn't get scared. I think she just wants to join in the game.

JUSTIN: Crikey, bub, no more Nickelodeon for you today. Now go and break a collarbone on something exciting, will you?

He ushers them out as the wind begins to pick up, carrying children's voices and laughter ...

SCENE FOUR

A children's playground. ABIGAIL *watches the kids play. A young kid shoves past and yells,* '**Weirdo!**' *Then a young man approaches her. He wears a smart school uniform.*

DYLAN: Hey.

ABIGAIL: Hey.

DYLAN: That dress is snatched.

ABIGAIL: Thanks. I think it's Victorian.

DYLAN: Yeah, Melbourne's heaps cooler than Sydney.

DYLAN *very awkwardly moves closer.*

Um … Can we try to … You know, like last time …

ABIGAIL: Um. Okay.

They kiss. It's awkward. '**It had the lingering pressure of a hairy sardine.**' *He ends by licking her eyebrow.*

You just licked my eyebrow.

DYLAN: Yeah. Did you like it?

ABIGAIL: No.

ABIGAIL *is shoved out of the way by a large schoolbag. It's* MEL. *She holds a phone.*

MEL: That is totally getting grammed, Dyl. Hashtag superspreader!

ACT ONE

DYLAN: Oh, hey Mel.
MEL: Who is she again?
ABIGAIL: Abigail Kirk.
MEL: Yeah, but what's your tag, Alison?
ABIGAIL: Oh no, I'm not on any—Can you please not post that?
MEL: Already out there, babes. Are you a tour guide?
ABIGAIL: Huh?
MEL: The dress.
DYLAN: Abigail likes to wear old stuff.
MEL: Oh, right.
DYLAN: She's from Tempe.
MEL: Tempe? Like the food? Random.
DYLAN: But she moved into the new Cumberland apartments a few months back.
MEL: Ew. Didn't homeless people live there?
ABIGAIL: That doesn't even make sense. And my mum and I don't *live* there. Mum and I got *put* there. My dad designed it. It's all part of his all-expenses-paid guilt trip through middle age.
MEL: Random. Well, I like your boots.
ABIGAIL: Thanks. I like your necklace.
MEL: My parents gave it to me when I got head prefect. It's Jesus being crucified. Wanna come to Westfield, Dyl? Got my mum's Land Rover.
DYLAN: Uh, sure. Abigail, do you / wanna—
MEL: There's probably not room for her. Sorry, Angela.
ABIGAIL: It's Abigail.
MEL: Whatevs. Don't be so sensitive. Come on, Dyl.

As she drags DYLAN *away …*

ABIGAIL: Mel. Don't move. You've got a spider on you.
MEL: What? Where? Get it. Kill it. Get it. Kill it. Kill it. Kill it.

ABIGAIL *gets the 'spider'. She holds it in her clasped hands.*

ABIGAIL: Got it.
MEL: Thank you.

VINNIE *has appeared beside* ABIGAIL. *He looks distressed.*

VINNIE: Abigail!
MEL: Have fun with your little friend, Alice. She is so weird …

She leaves with DYLAN.

VINNIE: I want to go home!
ABIGAIL: Vinnie, what's wrong?
VINNIE: They're gonna play Beatie Bow.
ABIGAIL: Beatie Bow?
VINNIE: The little furry girl, remember?

The children form a circle around a single child.

See? That's Mudda. Like a mummy.

One of the children makes the sound of a dog scratching. The children start to sing ...

CHILDREN: **Oh, Mudda, what's that? What's that?**
CHILD [MUDDA]: **Nothing at all ... The dog at the door ...**

Another child howls like the wind ...

VINNIE: Abigail, please let's go home!
ABIGAIL: Not yet, Vinnie.
CHILDREN: **Oh, Mudda, what's that? What's that?**
CHILD [MUDDA]: **The wind in the chimney, that's all, that's all.**

The wind picks up and the children all look around, warily.

VINNIE: Abigail, please ...
ABIGAIL: Shh, Vinnie.
CHILDREN: **Oh, Mudda, what's that? Can you see?**
CHILD [MUDDA]: **The cow in the byre ... The horse in the stall ...**
VINNIE: Abigail, she's coming. She's coming. The little furry girl!

He tugs at her desperately.

ABIGAIL: Vinnie, leave me *alone!*

BEATIE BOW *appears from the other side of the playground. She watches the game.*

VOICES: **Oh, Mudda, what's that in the shadows?**
CHILD: **A fox in its hole ... A hare in its burrow ...**

VINNIE *sees* BEATIE, *but* ABIGAIL *is busy admiring Mel's Jesus necklace that she has stolen. And her grandmother's watch.* VINNIE *wails softly into his hands.*

VOICES: **Oh, Mudda, I see something there!**

CHILD: **Close your eyes bairn, shhh shhh, there there …**

BEATIE points her finger at ABIGAIL *as a child appears covered in a white sheet.*

VOICES: **Oh, Mudda, what's that up ahead?!**
CHILD: **It's Beatie Bow! Back from the *dead*!**

The circle breaks and the children run, shrieking, taking ABIGAIL *and* VINNIE *with them.*

Once again, BEATIE BOW *disappears from view …*

SCENE FIVE

ABIGAIL *hums softly to herself. She is now in her bedroom, attaching the yoke to her green dress. She places the stolen crucifix necklace over the yoke.*

Meanwhile, KATHY *passes through the dark house with a man—* WEYLAND.

ABIGAIL*'s humming becomes the words of the children's song …*

ABIGAIL: **Oh, Mudda, what's that in the shadows?**
A fox in its hole … A hare in its burrow …

KATHY *and* WEYLAND *tiptoe through the house, a little tipsy.* ABIGAIL *sings on …*

Oh, Mudda, I see something there …

She hears something in the dark house …

Close your eyes bairn, shhh, there there …

She starts to tiptoe through the space …

Oh, Mudda, what's that up ahead …

ABIGAIL *sees* KATHY *and* WEYLAND *in a passionate embrace.*

Oh my God! *Mum! Dad?!*

KATHY *and* WEYLAND *stand before her in disarray.*

How long has this been going on?
WEYLAND: A couple of months.
ABIGAIL: *Months?!*
WEYLAND: We wanted to tell you, Lynette, / but—

ABIGAIL: It's *Abigail*. You two are disgusting.
KATHY: [*to* WEYLAND] We are disgusting. We shouldn't have had that extra bottle.
WEYLAND: We were celebrating! This is good, sweetheart!
ABIGAIL: Don't call me sweetheart.
WEYLAND: All of us back together again! Under the same roof!
ABIGAIL: All of us? Oh, is your girlfriend here too?
KATHY: That's all over now, Abigail—
ABIGAIL: Here I was thinking that you'd picked yourself up and moved on with some dignity, Mum—
KATHY: I am! / I did!
ABIGAIL: —left your law firm, started a new business, moved in here—
WEYLAND: Don't forget who got you this place, Lynette—
ABIGAIL: [*to* WEYLAND] Your company is letting us stay 'temporarily', *Weyland*. It's a perk of the job, like your girlfriend—
WEYLAND: She wasn't a perk. It was a very meaningful affair.
ABIGAIL: I was so proud of you, Mum, and the whole time you've been seeing this idiot behind my back!
KATHY: This idiot happens to be your father, Abigail!
ABIGAIL: What is *wrong* with you? Are you going through menopause or something?
KATHY: I'm forty-two! I'm in my bloody prime, aren't I, Weyland?
WEYLAND: You are. She is. Sweetheart—
ABIGAIL: *Don't* call me / sweetheart!
WEYLAND: Lynette, I promise it'll be different / this time—
ABIGAIL: My name is *Abigail*!

> WEYLAND *shakes his head—deflated. He's got nothing. He leaves.*

KATHY: Abigail. I know it isn't liberated. Not in the slightest. But even after what he did, even after letting time pass, I just can't seem to …

> *Beat.*

You've never been in love.
ABIGAIL: No, and I hope I never am, if it makes me act like you.
KATHY: Then you don't know how powerful it can be. Love. You don't know that yet. Whether it's the way I love him, or the way he loved her, or the way I love you. It's the most powerful thing in the world.

> *Beat.*

Abigail. Your dad has to move to Norway for work. He wants us to go with him and I've agreed—it's a good idea. We'd have to pack up the flat pretty fast—he's due there in a week. But at least we'll be together. A fresh start.

ABIGAIL: Did you say *Norway*? Mum, we've only just settled into The Rocks!

KATHY: You don't like it here, you tell me that all the time.

ABIGAIL: I'm not moving to Norway, Mum!

KATHY: They're very progressive in Scandinavia. Good schools. Very / open—

ABIGAIL: *I'm not moving to Norway!*

KATHY: *I can't just leave you here!*

    ABIGAIL *stops, stunned.*

What?

ABIGAIL: You're dumping me. For him.

KATHY: What? No. / I …

ABIGAIL: You're doing to me exactly what he did to you.

KATHY: Abby, it's not the same.

ABIGAIL: Yes it is, Mum! You're walking out on me!

KATHY: Oh, you're so bloody self-absorbed, Abigail! 'I hate this school, I hate that school, I don't fit in, I'm changing my name, I'm getting bullied!' Is it any bloody wonder?! Look at you! Why are you wearing a crucifix …?

ABIGAIL: Because you're not exactly working out as a responsible guide through life, Mum.

KATHY: Next Sunday I am flying to Norway with your father. The tickets are booked. Everything is in place. Are you coming with us or not? Abigail?

ABIGAIL: I don't want anything to do with either of you for the rest of my life.

    Beat.

Hurts, doesn't it?

SCENE SIX

ABIGAIL *sits under the Sydney Harbour Bridge as children's voices ring out in the distance.*

CHILDREN: **Oh, Mudda, what's that? What's that?**
Nothing at all. The dog at the door.
Oh, Mudda, what's that? What's that?
The wind in the chimney, that's all, that's all.

ABIGAIL *sings along numbly, stroking the yoke.*

ABIGAIL / CHILDREN: **Oh, Mudda, what's that? Can you see?**
The cow in the byre ... The horse in the stall.

Suddenly, BEATIE BOW *appears.* ABIGAIL *and* BEATIE *lock eyes.* ABIGAIL *stands, stunned. She keeps singing softly along with the tune.*

ABIGAIL / CHILDREN: **Oh, Mudda, what's that in the shadows?**
A fox in its hole ... A hare in its burrow.

ABIGAIL *waves to the strange little girl.*

ABIGAIL / CHILDREN: **Oh, Mudda, I see something there ...**

BEATIE BOW *waves back!* ABIGAIL *stops, stunned.*

ABIGAIL / CHILDREN: **Close your eyes bairn, shhh shhh, there there ...**

ABIGAIL *walks toward* BEATIE.

ABIGAIL / CHILDREN: **Oh, Mudda, what's that up ahead ...**
ABIGAIL: Are you the little furry girl?

BEATIE *gapes back at her, wide-eyed.*

CHILDREN: **It's Beatie Bow, back from the *dead*!**

ABIGAIL *reaches out a hand and touches* BEATIE. *The children scream.*

So does BEATIE. *So does* ABIGAIL. BEATIE *starts to run,* ABIGAIL *follows.*

ABIGAIL: Hey! Wait!

The Town Hall clock starts to chime ...

One ...

BEATIE *runs across a street.* ABIGAIL *follows, a car horn blares.*

Two ...

BEATIE *hurries up a steep staircase* **'between tall stone walls.'**
ABIGAIL *follows.*

ACT ONE 15

The Harbour Bridge looms behind them. A train clatters noisily.
Three ...

I only want to talk to you! Stop!

BEATIE *bounds up the steps to Harrington Street.*

Behind them, the Harbour Bridge starts to fade from view. Traffic sounds warp eerily.

In a maze of alleys, the shops and pubs become houses **'pressed close to the earth like lichen, with shingled roofs covered with moss.'**

Four ...

BEATIE *tries to hide behind a stone wall. The air seems thicker ... smoggier ...*

What are you running from?

The stone arch of The Cut on Argyle Street seems to close in and become narrower behind her.

Wait! I'm not going to hurt you!

BEATIE *runs toward Susannah Place.* ABIGAIL *follows, unaware that the Harbour Bridge is fading away above her.*

Five ...

ABIGAIL *sings out loudly, trying to stop her ...*

Oh, Mudda, what's that, what's that?!

Six ...

But she is answered by a sudden eerie silence. The street darkens around her.

The cobblestones beneath her feet are suddenly wet with sludge.

The path is lit only by **'glass-windowed lanterns which waved and waggled blue fishtails of flame.'** ABIGAIL *covers her mouth and nose from a growing stench.*

She turns in the street to see a world that was somehow familiar, and yet entirely unknown. **'She'd lost all power to move.'**

BEATIE *appears before her. The two girls stare at one another, face to face.*

BEATIE: Ye should ne'er hae followed me, ye silly wench!
ABIGAIL: Where am I? What is this place?

> But BEATIE *just shoves past* ABIGAIL, *to the edge of The Cut and* **'into the doorway of a corner house or shop, with a lighted window and a smell of burnt sugar.'**
>
> ABIGAIL *hurries after her, but as she gets to the door a huge man—* SAMUEL BOW—*appears in a long white apron. He brandishes a rusty scimitar, held high above his head.*

MR BOW: *Charge the heathen devils! The Rooshins is comin'! Hearts of oak—charge!*

> *He glares down at* ABIGAIL *and raises his scimitar to strike. She screams. Blackout.*

SCENE SEVEN

In darkness, voices whisper in a thick Scottish brogue ...

DOVEY: Is she the one, Granny? Has the time finally arrived?
GRANNY: My feelings are as confused as fairies in a fog, Dovey.
DOVEY: But do ye think she could be ... the Stranger?
GRANNY: 'Tis certain she's from a faraway land, but who isn't, around here? Time will tell if she is here to serve us or no'. For now, we'll just have to watch and wait.

> *The lights fade up.* ABIGAIL *stirs slightly as* DOVEY *and* GRANNY *tend to her.*

DOVEY: Her fever has broke. She's no' so burnin' now.

> **'Abigail was in neither a hospital nor her own home. The air was warm and stuffy. There was an open fire in the room and it was burning coal. The firelight leapt up, reflecting pinkly on the sloping ceiling.**
>
> **'Dovey had one of the sweetest faces she had ever seen, a young girl's, with a soft, baby's complexion,'** *save for a dark red burn that covered one cheek.*
>
> **'Granny had brown skin creased like old silk, with a sculptured smile on the sunken mouth. It was a composed, private face,**

with the lines of hardship and grief written on it. She wore a long black dress and white apron, and on her head was a huge pleated white cap with streamers.'

DOVEY *tends to* ABIGAIL*'s leg, which is raised on a pillow.*

She's quite the lady, Granny, no doubt. Her bracelet is made of the finest gold and has the hands of time on it. And she's one of God's children—Jesus Himself sits over her heart. And look at this skin—soft and plush, with nails as clean as Queen Victoria's own.

BEATIE *enters.*

BEATIE: She's no queen, Dovey. Queens dinnae smash through a family's front door at dennertime. She's a peedie whelp, is what she is.

ABIGAIL *rears slightly.*

DOVEY: Hush wi' that language, Beatie. She's wakening.

ABIGAIL: Argh! My foot! Oh my God!

GRANNY, DOVEY *and* BEATIE *gasp and cross themselves.*

BEATIE: Tole' ye she's a peedie whelp!

GRANNY *whacks* BEATIE *gently across the back of the head.*

GRANNY: Take a sup of posset, dearie, 'tis good for pain.

GRANNY *feeds* ABIGAIL *a sip from a mug.* ABIGAIL *retches, sickened.*

ABIGAIL: Where's my mum?

GRANNY: I'm sure she's not far away. Fear not—Granny's here, and Dovey and Beatie, and we'll no' leave ye, I promise.

BEATIE: She's not your granny, she's mine!

She is whacked again. ABIGAIL *sees* BEATIE.

ABIGAIL: You're the little furry girl …

DOVEY: Do ye know each other, Beatie?

BEATIE: Never seen her before in my lifetime. She's mad as a wet cat, this one!

ABIGAIL: What … What are you wearing? What am I wearing?

GRANNY: Yer dress was in tatters, bairn. Sodden through with all and whatnot. You'll feel better in a nightgown while ye get some rest.

DOVEY *puts something under* ABIGAIL*'s leg. She screams.*

ABIGAIL: What's that?
BEATIE: 'Tis a hot pig, daftie!
DOVEY: Beatie. Hush.
BEATIE: 'Tis a stone bottle filled with water. Took us an age to get it warm, so stop yer complainin'.
ABIGAIL: My foot is in agony. Oh my God …

BEATIE, DOVEY and GRANNY cross themselves again.

DOVEY: Ye wrenched yer ankle terrible bad when ye fell. We've put some comfrey paste on it to ease ye.
ABIGAIL: I didn't fall. Some drunk idiot with a sword knocked me over.
BEATIE: Don't ye be callin' me faither an eedjut.
GRANNY: Beatie.
BEATIE: He just has battle spells, is all.
ABIGAIL: Who *are* you?
BEATIE: I'm Beatie Bow.
ABIGAIL: That's not a name. That's a game.

BEATIE speaks through clenched teeth, warningly.

BEATIE: I ken that well enough, but it's my name—Beatrice May Bow—and although I may only be eleven years of age, I can still prog a fair punch in yer wee peedie puggy.

GRANNY whacks her again.

GRANNY: Beatie.
ABIGAIL: What the hell did you just say? What *is* this place?

She tries to get out of bed. They gently block her.

BEATIE: She's got more questions than Adam and Eve, this one.
GRANNY: Yer in the best bedroom of the Bow house.
DOVEY: Above the confectionery shop.
ABIGAIL: I mean … What language are you speaking? Where am I?
BEATIE: Have ye lost yer mind? It's the colony of New South Wales, of course!

ABIGAIL is growing increasingly distressed as her attempts to get out of bed are thwarted.

ABIGAIL: I have to go home. My mum will / be getting ready to—
GRANNY: Rest sure, my bonnie, that ye'll have yer mother as soon as we know where she lives and what name ye go by.

ACT ONE

ABIGAIL: We live in The Rocks!
GRANNY: *On* The Rocks.
ABIGAIL: My name is Abigail—
DOVEY: Abigail! That's a good Biblical name!
ABIGAIL: I thought it was a witch's name.
GRANNY: A witch? No. In the Lord's book, Abigail was a very wise prophetess.
DOVEY: She was also one of four of the most beautiful women in all the world.
BEATIE: She was the fourth. Of the four.
GRANNY: And she went on to become the wife of David.
DOVEY: David! Who slayed Goliath!
BEATIE: David had a lot of wives. He was quite the bodice buster.
GRANNY: Abigail is a good, holy name.
DOVEY: A good, holy name!
BEATIE: Aye, a good holy name. For a *witch*.
ABIGAIL: I'd like to go now, please—

> *She is stopped by a figure entering, covered by a dark blue sailor's coat and twittering.*
>
> *The only part visible is* **'a big brown hand, on the outstretched forefinger on which is perched a bird, its fingers a tinsel green.'**

BEATIE / DOVEY / GRANNY: *Judah! You're home!*

> BEATIE *pulls off the coat to reveal a young man with fair hair—* JUDAH. *He has* **'a square-cut jacket of dark blue, with metal buttons and crumpled white trousers.'** *He approaches* ABIGAIL, *holding the bird in front of him.*

JUDAH: Hello there, lassie. Would you know what this is?

> *He holds the bird out to her. She shakes her head, utterly confused.*

BEATIE: I do. 'Tis a hummingbird, Judah.
JUDAH: Aye, Beatie. [*To* ABIGAIL] She came from the Orinoco. I got her for a florin from a deep-water man. Did ye ever see aught as fine? They're magical creatures, hummingbirds. They can fly backwards and forwards and backwards again in the wink of an eye. And they're able to find the sweetest nectar even in the most bitter parts of the world.

He makes more whistling sounds. ABIGAIL *stares at him wide-eyed.*

ABIGAIL: I have absolutely no idea what is going on right now.

BEATIE: The bird isn't alive—me brother is makin' noises with his mouth.

JUDAH: Givin' away all me tricks, are ye, sister? Does Beatie want a beatin'?!

He chases her and she squeals. DOVEY *watches them, beaming.*

GRANNY: Careful, Judah. Beatie. Remember we have a lady present.

JUDAH *holds out his hands to an utterly confused* ABIGAIL.

JUDAH: Pick one!

BEATIE: Can I, Judah?

JUDAH: Ladies first, Beatie. Pick one, Abigail.

ABIGAIL *warily picks a hand.* JUDAH *reveals a sweet.*

'Tis a pink sugar mouse!

BEATIE: Our faither makes them in his confectionary shop downstairs! They're the best in all of Sydney Town!

JUDAH: Do ye fancy a nibble, Abigail?

GRANNY: It'll hurry the blood back to yer head.

ABIGAIL *stares at* GRANNY.

ABIGAIL: You look like Queen Victoria.

GRANNY *looks very pleased.*

GRANNY: Oh, ye're makin' me blush! Queen Victoria?! Do ye think so, lassie?

BEATIE: Queen Victoria's husband died of the typhoid!

GRANNY: She's a little stouter than I am, but I suppose there is a resemblance …

BEATIE: He was covered in red spots from heid to heel and then went completely barmy and died right there on the floor of Windsor Castle like a cockroach.

She demonstrates. It's graphic. JONAH *laughs.*

DOVEY: Beatie! What manners are they teaching you at the Ragged School?

Our queen's poor late husband was not a cockroach.

ABIGAIL: But … the Queen is Elizabeth.
GRANNY: Why, Good Queen Bess died hundreds of years ago, lass. Your mind's still on the wander.
ABIGAIL: I want to see where I am.

> *She goes to get up.*

JUDAH: Sure as your life, hen.

> *He swoops her into his arms.*

ABIGAIL: Put me down!

> *She hits him.* JUDAH *hurriedly places her back down, mortified.*

JUDAH: My apologies, Miss Abigail. I often have to carry ladies off the boats, you see. Gentlemen too, to be fair.
ABIGAIL: Well, I don't need to be carried by anyone. I can take care of myself. Thank you.

> ABIGAIL *stumbles awkwardly. As the family watch on, she redeems herself and walks painfully to take in the outside surrounds.* **'She looked out onto a gas-lit street, fog forming ghostly rainbows about the lamps. She had a wide view of thousands of smoking chimneys. The city had become dimmish blotches of light.'**

The Bridge has gone … And the freeway … The Opera—Where's the Opera House gone?
DOVEY: No opera in Sydney Town, Abigail. Although I would love to see such a spectacle, myself.
JUDAH: One day, Dovey. Promise.
ABIGAIL: Where are the roads? The trains, the planes? Where are the cars?

> *Her panic grows as she looks out the window in horror.*

What … What *year* is this?

> *She turns to the family who stare at her, wide-eyed.*

GRANNY: Why, it's 1873 in this year of our Lord and half gone already.

> ABIGAIL *stares back at them, horrified.* BEATIE *laughs and copies her.*

BEATIE: She looks like a muddle-headed wombat!
DOVEY: She's still all a-swither, poor lamb.

JUDAH: [*softly*] Granny. Do ye think this could be … who we've been waiting for?

GRANNY: Well, the job of a Stranger is to be strange …

They stare at her. ABIGAIL *stands awkwardly in the underwear, suddenly feeling quite naked.*

ABIGAIL: … Can I please have my dress back?

GRANNY: Rest a wee while, Abby, while we see to Uncle Samuel. Beatie, help our guest back to bed, seeing you're getting on so grand.

BEATIE *is all treacle as she assists* ABIGAIL *back to bed.*

BEATIE: Aye, Granny, I will. Come, Abigail. Let's get you off that sweet little foot.

As JUDAH, DOVEY *and* GRANNY *depart …*

JUDAH: Hold onto the hummingbird, Abigail. It'll share its nectar and have you healed in no time.

He makes the bird chirrup one last time.

When they've left, BEATIE *spins* ABIGAIL *roughly to face her, all smiles gone.*

BEATIE: Dunna tell Granny where you come from. Dunna breathe a word of it!

She'll say I have the Gift and I dinnae want the Gift! I didna mean tae bring ye here. I didna know it could even be done, heaven's truth!

ABIGAIL *stares at her, still coming to terms with her predicament.*

Promise me ye won't tell Granny! Honour bright! *Honour bright!*

ABIGAIL: Is it true? What they said? This is 1873?

BEATIE *grabs* ABIGAIL *and raises a fist.*

BEATIE: Say honour bright or I'll beat ye yeller and green!

ABIGAIL *suddenly turns on* BEATIE.

ABIGAIL: *You!* You did this to me!

BEATIE: 'Tisn't so! You chased me like a fox after a hare. It wunna my fault you got in Faither's way!

ABIGAIL: I have to go home! My mum will think I've run away!

BEATIE: I dunna ken where yer home even is! I didna mean to go there meself! It were the bairnies calling my name!

ABIGAIL: Tell me how to get home! I have to get back before Mum leaves for Nor / way—

BEATIE: One minute I was in the lane by the lamppost, and the next moment I was surrounded by giant shining towers, and a great archway goin' over the water, and strange carriages with ne'er a horse amongst them, and I was afeared out of my wits thinking my fever had returned, but then I heard the bairns calling my name, and they were playing a game we play around the streets here, except we call it Janey Jo.

> *She sings.*
>
> **Oh, Mudda, what's that? What's that?**
> **It's Janey Jo back from the *dead*!**

I tried to speak to one or two, but only you and that wee one with the yeller coat ever paid me any mind!

ABIGAIL: Vinnie …

> *She calls to The Rocks outside:*
>
> *Vinnie?! Mum?!*

BEATIE: What is the palm book they all read where you come from?

> *She demonstrates. She has misconstrued smart phones for tiny Bibles.*

They point out a lot of words. Is it one of the Gospels?

ABIGAIL: *Mum?!*

BEATIE: Yer all very devout, I must say. Everywhere I looked, there were people walkin' around, readin' their palm books and bumpin' into things.

ABIGAIL: Ow … my ankle …

> *She sits down, exhausted and in pain.* BEATIE *shakes her head, confused.*

BEATIE: So many strange things. A curved castle made of shells, and carriages spinning through the sky and all manner of people wearing tiny wee clothes and funny little masks and … That man with the big smiling mouth on the water— [*impersonating Luna Park*] —is he the King of Elfland?

ABIGAIL: There's no such thing as Elfland.

BEATIE: Green as a leek, you are. Of course there's an Elfland. That's where Granny's great-great-great-great-great-great-great-great-great granny first got the Gift. It's bonny, your home. Elfland.

ABIGAIL: It's not bloody Elfland! Now shut up and let me think!

BEATIE: Yer a right Lady Muckitty-Muck. Chasin' me here and takin' the best bedroom and not tellin' me nowt about how the Elffolk know my name. If you don't tell me, I'll shove that sugar mouse so far down your throat it'll make a nest in yer ribcage.

ABIGAIL: Just get me back to where I came from!

BEATIE: Ye cannae get ye back without yer dress!

ABIGAIL: Why not?

BEATIE: I don't know. Granny won't say. But ye won't get far without it.

ABIGAIL: You get me my dress back or I will call on the elves to come and get me themselves. And believe me, you do not want to see the Elf King angry.

>BEATIE*'s eyes widen in fear. Then ... she raises a fist to* ABIGAIL *and sneers furiously.*

BEATIE: Ye *are* a peedie whelp.

>ABIGAIL *raises a fist to* BEATIE, *just as fierce.*

ABIGAIL: No, Beatie. I'm a lady, remember? Now get me my goddamn dress.

>*The two of them glare at one another furiously. Then ... a sound. A child whimpering above.*

>*The two girls look up.*

What's that? What's that?

>BEATIE *takes her chance. She hurries out as the distraught cries continue.*

>ABIGAIL *listens, wide-eyed, as a sweet voice starts to sing 'Minnie o' Shirva's Cradle Song'* ...

DOVEY: **Da boatie sails an da boatie rowes,**
Dey set dir sails an dey hail dir towes,
Hush-a-baa-baa, me peerie lamb,
De faider is comin' awa fae fram ...

ACT ONE 25

ABIGAIL *darts wildly around the room, looking for some way to escape as the wails continue. Outside, Sydney Town darkens and citizens go about their nightly business. Amongst them is* KATHY, *wandering, humming her own tune ...*

ABIGAIL *peers at her desperately through the window ...*

ABIGAIL: Mum?! Mum ...? I'm up here! Mum!

KATHY *disappears as* DOVEY'S *sweet song continues on ...*

I don't know how I got here ...
How can it be ... 1873 ...?

DOVEY: **Da burnie rins an da burnie rowes**
Da lambs dey dance ower da hedder-knowes,
Hush-a-baa-baa, me treasure dear,
Dey'll naebody hurt thee whin Mam is near ...

The cries fade inside the house.

SCENE EIGHT

Morning. DOVEY *opens the curtains inside Abigail's room.* DOVEY *holds a smoking lavender sprig. A modesty room divider has been set up across the space.* DOVEY *peers at it awkwardly as she continues her song ...*

DOVEY: Are you alright back there, Abigail?
ABIGAIL: [*from behind the screen*] Yes. Fine.
DOVEY: Beatie will have quite the story to tell at the Ragged School today, I'm sure. An exotic princess showing up on our humble doorstep!
ABIGAIL: I'm not a princess.

ABIGAIL *appears from behind the screen and holds a chamber pot out to* DOVEY.

And I'm not exotic.

DOVEY *peers into the pot. She's impressed.*

DOVEY: Bonny!

She wafts the lavender around the room.

There now! All sweet again, ye are.

The two young women stare at one another. ABIGAIL *is uncomfortable in the nightdress.*

How do you feel this morning, Abby love?

ABIGAIL: Much better. Thank you for your hospitality. If you could just get me my dress, I can find my own way home.

DOVEY: It's only been a night since yer fright, Abby. Best rest yer wee ankle while ye can.

ABIGAIL: I'm fine. It doesn't hurt as much now.

DOVEY *stares at her wide-eyed.*

DOVEY: Your hair is as shiny as a thoroughbred.

ABIGAIL: Um. Thank you?

DOVEY: And you don't have a single freckle. I checked while you were sleeping.

ABIGAIL: Okay, please get me my dress.

DOVEY: I know what it is to have the cabin fever. I myself don't ever leave this house except for Sunday Mass. You may have noticed my scorched cheek—best not to fright people. You, though … yer so very pretty, Abigail. You deserve to be seen, in good time.

ABIGAIL: Please, I just need some fresh air.

She heads for the door. DOVEY *steps in her way.* GRANNY *enters.*

GRANNY: Fresh air on The Rocks! Ye'd get fresher air kissin' a dead trout, Abigail. Now, can ye remember anything more clear-like today, hen?

ABIGAIL: The same I told you yesterday. I'm Abigail Kirk. And I want to go home.

GRANNY: Where is home, child?

DOVEY: One of the Exotic Empires of the Orient, aye?

ABIGAIL: I told you. I live on Cumberland Street. In The Rocks.

GRANNY: You mean *on* The Rocks?

ABIGAIL: No. *In* The Rocks.

GRANNY: No-one lives *in* The Rocks. We all live *on* The Rocks. [*To* DOVEY] She's definitely not a local.

DOVEY: So you must be a Celestial from the Far East. Here to work as a parlour maid, perhaps, to support yer family back home?

ABIGAIL: I'm from out there. The Rocks. Sydney. And if I don't get back soon I won't *have* a family back home. Only bloody Norway. So please get me my dress.

DOVEY: I believe the dress was so stained with blood and dirt, Granny sent it next door to Johnny Whites the launder, did ye not, Granny?
GRANNY: Aye. I'm sure he'll have it back to ye soon looking good as new, Abigail. He works marvels, does Johnny Whites.
DOVEY: In the meantime, I've set ye out my finest skirt and bodice.

She hands some items to ABIGAIL *who realises something is amiss ...*

ABIGAIL: Where's my ... underwear?
DOVEY: Ye had hardly a thing for underclothes! A few queer rags and drawers the size of a babby's!
GRANNY: Now, slip your arms through here and I'll hook ye up.

ABIGAIL *smells the garment before her and winces slightly.*

ABIGAIL: How do I know your clothes aren't ... diseased? I don't know if my vaccinations cover this.

DOVEY *and* GRANNY *are stopped in their tracks.*

GRANNY: We bathe every Saturday night like clockwork, I'll have ye know, girl.
We are always clean and proper for the Sabbath.
DOVEY: And we boil our linen in vinegar and hang them out to sun-bleach every Monday.
GRANNY: We keep good and cleanly in this house. Even Johnny Whites himself admired my cuffs t'other day.

She peers into the chamber pot.

Oooh! Bonny! Come along now. Dress.

They help ABIGAIL *dress and keep chatting as they work ...*

Ye need not worry yerself, Abigail. We'll take care o' ye. We always do.
GRANNY / DOVEY: [*together*] That's the Tallisker way.
ABIGAIL: I thought your names were Bow.
DOVEY: Granny and I are Talliskers. She's my faither's mother. When my parents died in the Orkneys, Granny decided we would both emigrate to the colony of New South Wales to live with her daughter Amelia who had married an English soldier—Samuel Bow.
ABIGAIL: The crazy drunk man with the sword ...?
GRANNY / DOVEY: [*together*] Aye.

GRANNY: But alas, when we arrived, we found the household fraught with fever. My daughter Amelia died not long after we arrived, right there in that very bed.

ABIGAIL *looks at the bed, revolted.*

ABIGAIL: So … who is that sailor guy with the weird bird?

DOVEY: Oh! Uncle Samuel's eldest son. Judah. Beatie's brother. My cousin.

She beams.

We grew up together before he moved to the colonies. Spent our childhoods running through the Scottish heather, searching the great craigs for magic stones.

ABIGAIL: Magic stones?

GRANNY / DOVEY: [*together*] Aye.

DOVEY: The Orkney Islands were built by all manner of magical spirits many thousands of years ago. 'Tis the most ancient of lands.

ABIGAIL: Not as old as Australia, though.

DOVEY: God's pardon?

ABIGAIL: *This* land is one of the oldest in the world. We get taught that at school.

DOVEY: This land is not even a century, Abigail! There's a reason it's called *New* South Wales, ye know!

GRANNY: There she is. Bonny. Pretty as Princess Beatrice, herself.

DOVEY / GRANNY: [*together*] Oh, aye.

ABIGAIL *stands in **'a long dark serge over the blouse, a ribbon belt with a pewter buckle, knee high stockings of hand-knitted wool in circles of brown and yellow, and knitted slippers with fringed tops.'** Her hair is pulled back tightly.*

SAMUEL BOW *enters. **'He was the ruin of what had probably been a handsome trooper. He twisted his scarred hands in his apron.'** He speaks in an English Midlands accent.*

MR BOW: M … Miss. P-p-please / f-f-f-f-

ABIGAIL: Stay away. Don't come near me again.

MR BOW: Last night I-I-I thought I was back in the British cavalry. And I-I-I thought you was a Rooshin.

DOVEY: [*whispering*] Uncle Samuel fought in Crimea. Only some of him came back.

ACT ONE

MR BOW: I ... th-thought you was comin' to get me. Ye just popped out of nowhere.
ABIGAIL: So did you! With a bloody sword!
MR BOW: Please ... f-f-f-f-f-f ...

    ABIGAIL *turns to* GRANNY, *spooked by the strange man.*

ABIGAIL: I have to leave now. I need to get to Mum before Dad takes / her to—
GRANNY: Of course ye can leave, Abigail—as soon as Johnny Whites has yer dress spick and span. For now, it's inside the Bow house you stay. Now, Samuel, help our guest down the stairs while we freshen her bedclothes.
DOVEY: And mind, Uncle. She won't be carried.

    MR BOW *holds out a shaking hand.* ABIGAIL *begrudgingly accepts it.*

SCENE NINE

As MR BOW *helps* ABIGAIL *down the stairs, he sings 'Orra Bhonna Bhonnagan' ...*

MR BOW: **Orra bhonna bhonnagan**
    Orra bhonnagan a ghraidh
    Orra bhonna bhonnagan
    Theid thu togail a bhuntat

    DOVEY *joins the song as she tends to Abigail's bed and room.*

DOVEY / MR BOW: **Orra bhonna bhonnagan**
    Orra bhonnagan a ghraidh
    Orra bhonna bhonnagan
    Theid thu togail a bhuntat

    GRANNY *joins in the round as* MR BOW *helps* ABIGAIL *through the house and into the candy store.*

GRANNY / DOVEY / MR BOW: **O cha leig mi thu'n tobar**
    O cha leig mi thu'n traigh
    O cha leig mi thu'n tobar
    Theid thu togail a bhuntat
    O cha leig mi thu'n tobar

Outside, the streets bustle with activity. The Rocks citizens pick up the song, only they use the lyrics of 'The Rousay Lullaby' to join the round.

PEOPLE OF THE ROCKS: **Tarowdle dowdle dowdle dowdle dowdeeow
Tarowdle dowdle dowdle dowdle dowdeeow
Tarowdle dowdle dowdle dow and
Tarowdle dowdle dowdle dow
Tarowdle dowdle dowdle dowdle dowdeeow**

As BEATIE *shows her father how to curtsy with a book on her head,* ABIGAIL *peers out of the Bow shop door, watching in wonder as The Rocks hustles and bustles around her—street urchins and wares-sellers and top-hatted men and housemaids and ... a man laden with large stuffed sacks. One of the sacks reads 'Johnny Whites Laundry'.*

The man calls through the Bow shop window ...

JOHNNY WHITES: Hello, Beatie Bow.

BEATIE: Good morning, Johnny Whites.

As JOHNNY WHITES *lumbers away,* ABIGAIL *checks to see if* MR BOW *and* BEATIE *are watching and then hurriedly limps out of the door, following* JOHNNY WHITES *as the song continues.*

PEOPLE OF THE ROCKS: **Tarowdle dowdle dowdle dowdle dowdeeow
Tarowdle dowdle dowdle dowdle dowdeeow
Tarowdle dowdle dowdle dow and
Tarowdle dowdle dowdle dow
Tarowdle dowdle dowdle dowdle dowdeeow**

Meanwhile, BEATIE *and* MR BOW *realise* ABIGAIL *has absconded.*

BEATIE: She's bloomin' skedaddled, Da!

BEATIE *hurries out of the shop, furious and her father takes a surreptitious swig of rum. At the same time,* ABIGAIL *follows* JOHNNY WHITES *through The Rocks, ducking and weaving. Awestruck by the spectacle around her, but trying to keep up with the laundry man.*

ABIGAIL: Excuse me! Mr Whites? Mr Whites!

He doesn't look back. Exasperated, she yells loudly.

ACT ONE 31

Oy! Johnny Whites!

He finally stops and turns. ABIGAIL *stares at him, panting. He looks familiar ...*

Sorry ... *warami*?

He looks surprised, then sizes her up.

JOHNNY WHITES: *Warami. Nǐ hǎo ma?*

ABIGAIL: No, I'm not from—Doesn't matter. I think you've got something of mine in that bag of yours.

JOHNNY WHITES: Oh yeah? And which bag do you reckon, missy?

ABIGAIL: I'm not sure. But you've got my dress. And I want it back now.

JOHNNY WHITES: Ah. What colour is this dress?

ABIGAIL: Green. With a lace collar.

JOHNNY WHITES: Green, hey?

He thinks, still sizing up the strange girl before him.

Sorry, miss. Only whites in here today.

He disappears into the crowd as they sing on loudly ...

PEOPLE OF THE ROCKS: **Tarowdle dowdle dowdle dowdle dowdeeow**
Tarowdle dowdle dowdle dowdle dowdeeow
Tarowdle dowdle dowdle dow and
Tarowdle dowdle dowdle dow
Tarowdle dowdle dowdle dowdle dowdeeow

ABIGAIL *is furious. She starts to steal things from people as they pass. An apple from a cart.*

A man's hat. A walking stick ... She gets more and more brazen as BEATIE *catches sight of her from afar.*

BEATIE: Oh my stars!

BEATIE *follows* ABIGAIL *as she steals her way through The Rocks.*

PEOPLE OF THE ROCKS: **You shall not go to the well,**
You shall not go to the shore
You shall not go to the well,
You shall lift the potatoes
You shall not go to the well,
You shall not go to the shore

> **You shall not go to the well,**
> **Go and lift the potatoes**

BEATIE grabs ABIGAIL.

BEATIE: What are ye doing outside, ye daft wench?!

ABIGAIL: I saw Johnny Whites! I tried to get my dress back!

BEATIE: Looks like ye got more than a dress there. Bin here one day and yer a bloomin' bushranger, Abigail?

ABIGAIL: They're souvenirs. This is The Rocks, isn't it?

BEATIE: Do ye want to get yeself hauled off to Darlinghurst Gaol? Ye'll be hanging in the gallows by supper time, ye peedie whelp. Now, away wi' ye!

She drags ABIGAIL *back through The Rocks, which is filled with the song.*

PEOPLE OF THE ROCKS: **You shall not go to the well**
You shall not go to the shore
You shall not go to the well
Go and lift potatoes

SCENE TEN

Silence. GRANNY *stands sternly in the Bow kitchen, staring at a defiant* ABIGAIL. BEATIE *watches on, wide-eyed.* DOVEY *waits quietly nearby.*

GRANNY: You were told to stay inside, child.

ABIGAIL: I just went to find my dress. And I'm not a child, I'm sixteen.

GRANNY: Yer dress is being laundered by Johnny Whites. I told ye that.

ABIGAIL: Beatie told me I need that dress to get home!

GRANNY: There'll be no more talk of that dress. Understand?

ABIGAIL: This is … kidnapping by laundry. This is definitely against the law.

GRANNY: We live by different laws on The Rocks, Abigail. I'm telling you, girl, you must not leave this house.

A wailing comes from upstairs. They all look up.

ABIGAIL: What *is* that noise?

DOVEY: The wind in the chimney that's all, that's all.

ACT ONE

GRANNY *places a large Bible on the table.*

GRANNY: The Sermon on the Mount should make up for today's mischief. Ye can read, can't you, girl?

ABIGAIL: Of course I can. I've been going to school for twelve years.

BEATIE: Twelve years? What's taking you so long?

DOVEY: Ye can read? I may answer to the name Dorcas Tallisker but I've no clue how to spell it except as a cross.

GRANNY: Perhaps readin' the Good Book will remind ye of yer purpose here, Abigail.

She stares pointedly at ABIGAIL *who just stares back, utterly confused.*

Let's see to that noisy chimney flue, shall we, Dovey? Read, girls! God's tappin' his foot.

ABIGAIL *watches warily as* GRANNY *departs with* DOVEY.

ABIGAIL: Your grandmother is completely bizarre.

BEATIE: Oh, you don't know the half of it.

She grumpily opens the Bible, muttering to herself.

Sermon on the Mount. It's longer than a month of Sundays. 'Blessed are the poor, blessed are the mourners, blessed are the meek.' I'd rather read the part where King Herod's tadger falls off from the scabies.

The wailing echoes once more through the house.

ABIGAIL: Beatie. Who keeps making that noise? I know it's not the chimney.

BEATIE: Just shut yer bloomin' gob and read the Beatitudes! God's waitin'!

ABIGAIL: Beatie, can't you just think for yourself instead of relying on all these Gods and elves and sermons and spells to tell you how to live?

BEATIE: Well, I'd *like* to think for meself, but I need to put more in here [*tapping at her head*] to do so! If I had my way, I'd be learnin' Greek and Latin and Geography and Algebra like the *boys*. I'd be studyin' the sciences like Charles Darwin or inspectin' apples like Isaac Newton or I'd be writin' poetry like George Eliot. I want to read more than just the Good Book. I want to read *great* books. I want to *write* my own book—a great big book. And yet I'll never. Those boys at the Ragged School will get to all the books afore me and they're a bunch of peedie mumble-pates.

ABIGAIL: Why don't you just join their classes?

BEATIE: Because I'm a girl, that's why, and girls cannae be proper scholars. Girls cannae be proper anything! We're not allowed to leave a mark of ourselves except maybe in a few babbies or etched into a gravestone, buried underneath our husband.

Beat.

And that's why I want to know how those bairns know my name, Abigail. They were *singin'* my *name*! So I must be doin' somethin' right if even the bairns of Elfland know Beatie Bow. Or maybe I'm doin' somethin' terribly wrong and I'll be forever remembered the same way as Eve and her apple, or Jezebel and her face paint, or Delilah and her scissors!

ABIGAIL: Okay. Alright. *Quid pro quo.*

BEATIE: What?

ABIGAIL: *Quid pro quo.*

BEATIE: Is that Latin? Ye know I don't speak bloomin' Latin, ye peedie show-off.

ABIGAIL: It means let's do a swap. I'll tell you the truth about Elfland if you agree to help me get out of here.

Beat.

BEATIE: The dear God help me if Granny kens what I'm doin'. She's dead set on your stayin' because she thinks you're the Stranger.

She gasps and covers her mouth.

It fell out of me gob again!

ABIGAIL: What do you mean I'm the 'Stranger'?

BEATIE: It dinnae matter now, because you have my word. When yer ankle is healed, I'll get you to Harrington Street. To the lamppost.

ABIGAIL: With my dress?

BEATIE: With yer bleedin' dress, Lady Muckitty-Muck. But now you have to give me your part of the deal. Prid pro woe. Quid prick toe. Ugh. Honour bright?

ABIGAIL: Honour bright.

BEATIE: Right. Tell me about Elfland.

ABIGAIL: Elfland—where I come from—is *this* place but a hundred and fifty years from now. It's still The Rocks, Sydney, but it's older than now ... and yet somehow younger. Do you understand?

BEATIE: No.

ABIGAIL: The big towers you saw are *skyscrapers* where people do their work, make their money. Some of them even have houses inside them where people live, like me and my mum. The curved castle made of shells that you saw is the *Opera House*, where people sing and dance and spend too much money on wine. The horseless carriages are *cars*—they take us across the big road over the water, the *Harbour Bridge*—and even further if we like, unless the borders are closed. The carriages in the sky are *airplanes* that fly us all over the world. To Scotland. Vietnam. America. Norway ... The palm books are *phones*—like letters, but we don't have to mail them. We can just speak to anyone we like through them. We can hold that person right there in our hand and they can hold us in theirs.

BEATIE: You can see anyone anywhere? Even Heaven?

ABIGAIL: Well, no. Anywhere with good reception.

BEATIE: Oh. Well, I don't need a palm book to hold someone in me hand. Look.

She gets something from her pocket—a locket. She opens it and takes out a lock of ribboned hair.

'Tis a lock of me ma's hair. I keep it in her pocket mirror. She told me before she passed away that whenever I wanted to see her, I only had to hold her hair in one hand and look at my reflection in the other.

She does. Then snaps it shut suddenly.

And what about the elves? In your time.

ABIGAIL: The elves are just ... humans. All living together on this little patch of land. It's not Elfland. It's just The Rocks. Sydney. The year 2021.

A moment of silence ... and then BEATIE *hits* ABIGAIL.

BEATIE: You're a damned leear! Such things inna possible, except in Elfland!

ABIGAIL: Ow! Well, I wouldn't have thought this place would be possible either! Not in my worst dreams.

BEATIE: What's the matter with here then?
ABIGAIL: Uh, it smells like faeces—horse *and* human; you can't move in these ridiculous clothes; they won't let a girl get a proper education; inebriated men just roam the streets with swords; I suspect everyone's even more racist than where I come from, and that's saying something; everything tastes like mutton; and you can't open a window for fear of dying of some kind of plague or pox or fever.
BEATIE: [*shocked*] Don't folk die of those things in your time?

> ABIGAIL *gives an awkward shrug.*

Then Mamma would still be alive and Gibbie wouldn't be so sickly …
ABIGAIL: Who's Gibbie?

> BEATIE *starts to cry.* ABIGAIL *takes the opportunity* …

Beatie, my dad is taking my mum away on Sunday. That's only a few days away. She'll leave without me if I don't go back. And I miss her. You know what it's like to miss your mum, don't you?
BEATIE: Of course I do!
ABIGAIL: My mum is my only real friend in the whole world. And until recently I was her only friend too. So to help me get back to her, you need to tell me more about why I'm even here. What is this business about me being the 'Stranger'? And what is this 'Gift' everyone talks about?

> *The wailing from upstairs begins again, startling them both.* BEATIE *pulls away, terrified.*

BEATIE: No. I've changed my mind. I cannae help ye.
ABIGAIL: But you promised you'd take me to Harrington Street! The lamppost! Honour bright, you said!
BEATIE: No! I dinnae care about Elfland anymore! And I dinnae want the Gift anymore! And I dinnae mean to kill me ma!

> *She clamps her hand over her mouth in horror, then runs away.*
>
> ABIGAIL *cries out in frustration and buries her head in her hands.*
>
> *A figure covered in a white linen blanket makes its way down the stairs, ghost-like and wailing.*

GIBBIE: Boo!

> ABIGAIL *screams. The creature removes the blanket. Revealed is a young boy.* '*He was like a small wizened monk. His head had been shaved. It was bony, bumpy and bluish.*' ABIGAIL *gapes at him.*

Mercy on me! You're as plain as a toad.

> *He approaches her.*

Hello. I'm Gilbert Samuel Bow. You may have heard me wailin' in torment.

> *He offers his hand instead.* ABIGAIL *shakes it reluctantly.*

You'll want to wash that hand, girly. [*Cough*] I'm riddled with contagion. If I live to my next birthday, it'll be quite the miracle. Now would you like to kiss my sweet, uncorrupted cheek before I receive my angel wings?

ABIGAIL: Absolutely not.

> *And she pushes past him back upstairs.*

SCENE ELEVEN

JOHNNY WHITES *enters, singing 'Mo Nighean Donn', as he hangs out radiantly white laundry. He sends his song to the east with a gesture.*

JOHNNY WHITES: **Washing Day is here again**
And I wish that you were too
Mo Nighean Donn hoo-roo hoo-roo
My brown-haired girls, hoo-roo
ALL: **Washing day, hoo-roo hoo-roo**
Washing day, hoo-roo hoo-roo
Washing day, hoo-roo
JOHNNY WHITES: **Today's the day The Rocks need me**
And I know that you do too
Mo Nighean Donn, hoo-roo hoo-roo
My brown-haired girls, hoo-roo
ALL: **Brown-haired girls, hoo-roo hoo-roo**
Brown-haired girls, hoo-roo hoo-roo
Brown-haired girls, hoo-roo

JOHNNY WHITES: **Wash those dresses, scrub those coats**
I will do it all for you
Mo Nighean Donn, hoo-roo hoo-roo
My brown-haired girls, hoo-roo
ALL: **Brown-haired girls, hoo-roo hoo-roo**
Brown-haired girls, hoo-roo hoo-roo
Brown-haired girls, hoo-roo
JOHNNY WHITES: **My brown-haired girls, hoo-roo …**

> ABIGAIL *calls to him from her window, ruining his reverie.*

ABIGAIL: *Warami* again, Johnny Whites.
JOHNNY WHITES: *Warami* again, strange-dress girl.
ABIGAIL: My name is Abigail Kirk.
JOHNNY WHITES: Where you from, Abigail Kirk?
ABIGAIL: The Rocks.
JOHNNY WHITES: Hah. Me too.
ABIGAIL: Have you cleaned my dress yet?
JOHNNY WHITES: Can you pay for it yet?
ABIGAIL: I don't have any money.
JOHNNY WHITES: Then it's not ready yet.

> ABIGAIL *remembers …*

ABIGAIL: You can have my grandmother's watch. It's gold.
JOHNNY WHITES: I don't dig anymore.
ABIGAIL: My necklace, then? It's a cross.
JOHNNY WHITES: Not a follower of that fella.
ABIGAIL: There's twenty dollars in my pocket. You can have it if it's still there.
JOHNNY WHITES: Oooh. Twenty dollars?
ABIGAIL: Yes. In the dress.
JOHNNY WHITES: Spanish dollars? American dollars? Norwegian dalars?
ABIGAIL: Australian dollars. Twenty of them.
JOHNNY WHITES: Ah. Australian dollars. Them holey ones that Macquarie fella came up with when he landed here in his big boat.
ABIGAIL: Sorry, what?
JOHNNY WHITES: You know that Macquarie fella! *Everyone* knows that Macquarie fella. He won't let us bloody forget him! Macquarie Street, Lake Macquarie, Macquarie River, Lachlan River, Fort Macquarie,

ACT ONE

Port Macquarie, every-bloody-sort Macquarie. And when he's not naming places after himself, he names them after his wife! Elizabeth Street. Elizabeth Bay. Lady Macquarie's Road. Mrs Macquarie's Chair ...

He keeps hanging out his washing.

They used to have other names, those places. Special names. Wish I could remember them. My grandmother would've known, but she was killed by orders of, guess who, Governor Macquarie. Which reminds me, any pounds, sovereigns or shillings, in your special dress, Abigail Kirk? 'Cos, strange as it is, that's what this 'hostile native' would prefer to deal in instead of any dumped dollars from that 'Father of Australia' Macquarie.

ABIGAIL: No. I don't have anything.

JOHNNY WHITES: And I don't have your dress. Too busy dealing with this load.

ABIGAIL: But I need it. If I don't have it then I'm bloody stuck here.

She starts to cry. JOHNNY WHITES *sends a handkerchief to her via his clothesline.*

JOHNNY WHITES: Take a hanky, Abigail Kirk. Tears don't get you nowhere in this place.

She takes the handkerchief from his line.

See how white it is?

He closes his window. ABIGAIL *looks at the street around her. Composes herself.*

ABIGAIL: I can work out how to get back. I don't need my dress. Or Beatie.

She takes in the streets below.

I think that could be Cambridge Street ... Which makes that Argyle Street ... Circular Quay and George Street are down there. Barangaroo is that way. So Harrington Street must be ...

A voice rings out. It's Kathy's song, only this time with words ...

SPAEWIFE: **O, I wad like to ken—to the beggar wife says I—**

ABIGAIL *clambers hurriedly out of her window onto the precarious roof outside.*

A cloaked woman passes below. 'A dark-brown braid fell over her left shoulder almost to her waist. Her hands were red and chapped. She wore a coarse ankle-length black skirt and a white apron.' She is singing the song.

SPAEWIFE: **The reason o' the cause an' the wherefore o' the why ...**
ABIGAIL: Mum? Is that you?! I'm coming! I'm five minutes from home! Can you hear me, Mum?

GRANNY watches from afar, unseen, as does BEATIE from another space. ABIGAIL slips a little as she tries to watch the strange woman pass. GRANNY reaches out a hand and magically stops ABIGAIL's fall. BEATIE watches on, unseen and terrified.

SPAEWIFE: **Why sae many of life's riddles brings the tear into my e'e.**
ABIGAIL: Five minutes and a hundred and fifty years ...
SPAEWIFE: **It's gey an' easy spierin', says the spae-wife to me ...**

SCENE TWELVE

ABIGAIL *and* GIBBIE, BEATIE, GRANNY, DOVEY, JUDAH *and* MR BOW *sit at a table in the kitchen. They are all praying, except* ABIGAIL.

GRANNY: Bless, O Father, Thy gifts to our use and us to Thy service; for Christ's sake. Amen.
ALL: [*except* ABIGAIL] Amen.

They start eating from soup bowls.

GIBBIE: I been thinking on my funeral, family. Six black horses I'll have, with deep purple ostrich plumes. And four men in tall hats with black streamers. And a dead cart covered in flowers.

They all go to eat. But GIBBIE *continues and they put their spoons down.*

Daisies—white—for my youthful purity. One single *crimson* rose for mourning. And forget-me-nots, so that you may never, ever, ever, ever, ever, ever, ever, ever, ever forget me.

They go to eat again. They get a mouthful in when ...

Snip off a lock of what hair I have so that you may share it among you and wear it over your hearts to remember the sinless babe returning to the bosom of his dead mother.

ACT ONE

As GIBBIE *goes to speak on ...*

ABIGAIL: You could just get cremated and save everyone the bother.

> *Everyone stares at her in horror. Except* MR BOW *who just keeps eating.*

We got Pop back in a plastic urn and then sprinkled him on his favourite golf course. Heaps easier.

GIBBIE: Such strange words you speak. Not proper English like the rest of us.

ABIGAIL: My deepest apologies, Gibbie. I'll speak more clearly. Where is my dress?

> *She glares at* DOVEY *and* GRANNY.

DOVEY: I ... believe Johnny Whites still has / it—

ABIGAIL: You sure do lie a lot for a Christian, Dovey.

> *Everyone gasps.*

BEATIE: That's my cousin yer talkin' about there, Abigail.

ABIGAIL: Johnny Whites told me today he's never seen my dress.

GIBBIE: I might just have some more broth for my weakening blood.

> *He helps himself.*

ABIGAIL: I've been here too long already. I have to get home. Give me my dress. *Now!*

GRANNY: Yer dress was burned, Abigail.

GIBBIE: Ooooohhh!

ABIGAIL: You *burned* my dress?

GRANNY: Threw it on the fire the very night you arrived. It was in no condition to be worn again. Now enough of such vain chatter—yer supper is getting cold.

> ABIGAIL *picks the soup pot off the table and empties its contents onto the floor.*

ABIGAIL: You ruin my dress, I ruin your supper.

> *They all stare at her, stunned.* JUDAH *laughs and* DOVEY *casts him an admonishing glance.*

GIBBIE: That's all the sustenance I had today! I'll be meetin' my maker by mornin'!

> GRANNY *rises from the table, softly reciting a chant.*

GRANNY: **Is tu gleus na Mnatha Sithe,**
        Is tu beus na Bride bithe,
        Is tu creud na Moire mine,
        Is tu gniomh na / mnatha Gréig
DOVEY: Oh, ye've risen the spirits in Granny, Abby!

    GRANNY *focuses on* ABIGAIL, *her eyes widening terrifyingly ...*

GRANNY: **Thine is the skill of the Fairy Woman,**
        Thine is the faith of Mary the mild,
        Thine is the virtue of Bride the calm,
        Thine is the tact of the women of Greece,
        Thine is the beauty of Emir the lovely,
        Thine is the courage of Maebh the strong,
        Thine is the charm of Binne-bheul,
        Thou heard the call of Spaewives all …

She raises her arm and points at ABIGAIL.

        Thou came to the door of The Tallisker clan,
        Thou art The Stranger. *Sit thee down!*

An unseen force shoves ABIGAIL *down.*

ABIGAIL: How did you do that?
BEATIE: The Gift.
JUDAH: The Prophecy.
DOVEY: Is it time, Granny?
GIBBIE: Oh, I can feel my spirit leavin' my poor wee body.
GRANNY: Ye are the Stranger, are ye not?
ABIGAIL: Not as strange as you lot.
GRANNY: Ye come with a message for this family?
ABIGAIL: Yes I do. You're all a bunch of lunatics.
GRANNY: Where have ye come from, Stranger? Are ye a sister Spaewife? Do you possess the Gift as well?
ABIGAIL: I don't know what you're talking about. I'm here because … Because …

    ABIGAIL *looks at a terrified* BEATIE. MR BOW *suddenly stands and raises his spoon high.*

MR BOW: *It was my Melia! Give 'er back, you Rooshin bastard!*
GIBBIE: Oh, blimey! Now Dada's having a battle spell!

ACT ONE

MR BOW: *Where's my wife, you red heathen? I'm gonna slice you from arsehole to brow!*

They all try to settle him, but to no avail. He grabs GIBBIE *and brandishes his spoon.*

Where did ye hide her, ye little Rooshin bastard?!

GIBBIE: He's gonna spoonfeed me to my Maker!

MR BOW *throws* GIBBIE *aside.*

MR BOW: *Hearts of oak, fellas! Charge!*

He swings his spoon, wild and violent. JUDAH *steps in suddenly.*

JUDAH: *Soljer! Stand down!*

MR BOW *stops suddenly.*

Lay down your arms, man. Captain's orders!

MR BOW *lowers the sword.*

Good job, soljer. Good job.

MR BOW *sinks to the ground, looking around, confused.*

MR BOW: Did ye see how many I stuck, Cap'n? Can't see the field for the bowels and entrails. I did that. I did that.

JUDAH: Aye, soljer. Ye did. Queen Victoria will reward ye well on yer return home. Home now, Da. Shhh. Shhh.

He has wooed his father back to reality.

MR BOW: [*muttering groggily*] Melia … Melia …

GRANNY: He's been on the wet. Douse him in the copper, Judah. Dovey, get Gibbie to bed. Leave me with the girl.

MR BOW *mutters under his breath as* JUDAH *helps him away.* GIBBIE *gasps for breath dramatically as* DOVEY *helps him upstairs.*

GIBBIE: I can hear Jesus and his lambs callin' me! 'Come to me, Gibbie! [*He bleats like a sheep.*] Come to me …'

BEATIE *watches from the corner, wide-eyed and silent, as* GRANNY *stands over* ABIGAIL.

GRANNY: Abigail Kirk. You are the Stranger and 'twas the Gift that brought ye to us.

ABIGAIL: I'm telling you, I don't have any kind of power. I never have in my life!
GRANNY: You are here to save this family.
ABIGAIL: What? How?
GRANNY: That remains to be seen. But without you, we cannae survive. And without that dress, ye cannae get home. So ye best get used to it, child. Until you use your Gift to save this family … on The Rocks is where ye stay. Now clean up this mess.

> *She leaves.* ABIGAIL *shakes her head, tearful. She glares at* BEATIE.

ABIGAIL: I have to tell them it was you, Beatie. I didn't get here by myself.
BEATIE: No! That's our secret! I'll get ye back. I promise.
ABIGAIL: When?! It's almost the weekend!
BEATIE: Tomorrow. It's market day. I'll say I needed yer help with carryin' the load and that I lost ye in the crowd.
ABIGAIL: I don't trust you, Beatie.
BEATIE: Well, yer going to have to. Because there's nothin' I want more than fer you to go back to where ye came from, Abigail.
ABIGAIL: If you don't get me home tomorrow, I'll tell Granny the truth—that it was *you* who brought me here, Beatie Bow. *You're* the one with the Gift. Not me.

> ABIGAIL *leaves.* BEATIE *opens her pocket mirror and takes out her mother's lock of hair.*
>
> *She sings forlornly as she strokes it across her cheek.*

BEATIE: **Come to me, Ma …**
Please come to me …

SCENE THIRTEEN

A new day in The Rocks. A Jew's harp twangs as the dawn rises.
MR BOW *appears in the shop, in an apron. He starts to stir his cauldron.*
DOVEY *hands* ABIGAIL *an apron in the store.*
JUDAH *hurries through on his way to the docks and smiles at her coyly. She can't help but return it, awkwardly self-aware.*

BEATIE *and* ABIGAIL *sweep the store with brooms as the reel continues softly.*

MR BOW: *Man your stations, girls!* Bow's Confections open for business! Bow's Confections open for business!

    ABIGAIL *is hurried behind the counter to serve as* JOHNNY WHITES *enters.*

JOHNNY WHITES: Sweethearts.
ABIGAIL: What … What did you call me?
JOHNNY WHITES: I didn't call you anything. I asked for a bag of sweethearts.

    MR BOW *hurries over and passes him a bag.*

MR BOW: Here you are, Johnny. Sweethearts for the children.

    JOHNNY WHITES *takes them and passes* MR BOW *a coin.*

No, my friend. On the house.
JOHNNY WHITES: Found that dress yet, Abigail Kirk?
ABIGAIL: It got incinerated. So don't bother keeping an eye out for it.
JOHNNY WHITES: I wasn't. Thank you, Mr Bow.

    JOHNNY *leaves the money anyway.* MR BOW *speaks softly.*

MR BOW: Johnny buys sweethearts for his children. They were taken away after his wife passed. But he still buys them sweethearts every week, like clockwork.
ABIGAIL: What are sweethearts?
MR BOW: Messages of love. They're a very special confection of affection. I inscribe them meself.

    He shows her some sweethearts.

Amelia. Amelia. Amelia.
BEATIE: Amelia was me ma.
MR BOW: She's my lost sweetheart. And Johnny has his. I write their names on every heart so that we may never forget. See?

    As he shows her, ABIGAIL *ducks away.*

ABIGAIL: Beatie, you *promised* you'd take me to the markets today.
BEATIE: That I *did*, Abigail. Da, stop yer gabbin' and let Abbie out fer a wee while. I need her to help me at the markets.

MR BOW: A sweetie for my Beatie?

BEATIE: Da, I'm eleven. I'm too old for bloomin' sweethearts. But sure, if I must.

She takes one and drags ABIGAIL *outside.*

Come, Abby.

MR BOW's smile fades and he takes a surreptitious swig of booze in his shop.

Outside, the reel gets wilder and wilder. ***'It was a fine day. People were out in crowds. Wheeled racks of tattered garments outside, the cobbler with a tall Wellington boot hung as a sign above his door, the itinerant cooks with their charcoal braziers—cooking and selling sausages, scallops, baked potatoes, haddocks, chitterlings—positioned every few yards along Argyle and Windmill streets.'*** ABIGAIL *stumbles from stall to stall, marvelling at the goods.* **'A man passes. He wears a dozen hats, one on top of the other.'**

HARRY THE HAT MAN: Tanner heach! Hats all clane! / Tanner hats! All / clane!

CHARLIE THE CHESTNUT SELLER: Hot chestnuts! All hot! / Get yer chestnuts, roasted and hot!

TRIXIE THE TRIPE SELLER: 'Ot and juicy tripe! Slaughtered yesterday, / bled this morn, dinner tonight! Juicy tripe!

BERTHA THE BOOK MERCHANT: Books! Books! Get yer books! We got Dickens, we got Darwin, / we got Eliot, we got bargins!

FERDIE THE FRUIT SELLER: China pears! Windsor apples! / China pears! Windsor apples!

OLIVE THE OIL SELLER: Lamp oil, cheapest and sweetest in town! We got whale, we got seal! Cheapensweet! Cheapensweet!

The reel is wild as the full gamut of Rocks locals fill the streets, from every walk of life.

Sailors and soldiers and drunks and shopkeepers and launderers shopping, fighting, laughing and dancing to the wild reel. ABIGAIL *can't help but get involved—surreptitiously stealing a book.*

Then ... a crack of thunder. Rain pours. The sky darkens. Everyone scurries.

ACT ONE

BEATIE *and* ABIGAIL *huddle under a discarded* Sydney Morning Herald.

ABIGAIL: Right. Get me out of here, Beatie. Quick. While no-one's around.

BEATIE: I'll do my best, but I cannae promise anything without the dress.

ABIGAIL: Beatie. My mum is leaving in three days. I have to get back to her now.

BEATIE: And I want ye to go now! It's just … using the Gift takes a lot out of a wee lassie.

ABIGAIL: Well, what if the wee lassie had these to sweeten the deal?

She pulls out the book. BEATIE's *eyes widen.*

BEATIE: George Eliot. Where did ye get that?!

ABIGAIL: I inherited it. And now I bequeath it to you.

BEATIE *reaches for it slowly … Then* ABIGAIL *pulls away sharply.*

But only if you promise you can get me home.

BEATIE: Of course I can! I'm the one with the bloomin' Gift, am I not?

ABIGAIL *passes* BEATIE *the book.*

The street lamp on Harrington Street is just up that pathway. Walk into the mist and I'll say a magic spell and ye'll be on yer way.

ABIGAIL: About time. Goodbye, Beatie.

BEATIE: Goodbye, Abigail.

They shake hands awkwardly, then … BEATIE *raises her hands in a kind of gawkish spell …*

Drums and trumpets, harps and fiddles
Mystic cards for solving riddles
Owls and geese and Dutch dragoons
Tigers, Frenchmen and baboons …

ABIGAIL *walks uncertainly into the mist. She calls back as she peers into the darkness.*

ABIGAIL: Baboons? Are you sure you know what you're doing?

BEATIE: Of course I'm sure! Just keep walking!

She keeps reciting. ABIGAIL *walks on …*

By the power vested in me
Underneath yond lamp you see

I beseech all the elves to take Abigail home
To her own place in time ... and leave me alone.
> ABIGAIL *calls out.*

ABIGAIL: It's so dark. Beatie, it doesn't look like the way I came—
> *She turns back, but* BEATIE *has disappeared.* ABIGAIL *is left on the quiet, misty street.*

Beatie? Beatie!
> *From afar, somewhere through space and time,* KATHY *appears humming her tune ...*

Mum. I'm coming ...
> ABIGAIL *starts to follow.* KATHY *moves further away, humming her tune ...*

Mum! *Wait! Mum! I'm here!*
> *Silence.* KATHY *is gone.*

Mum? / *Mum?!*
> *From out of nowhere, ominous whispers overlap one another.* ABIGAIL *runs deeper into The Rocks, up alleys and down cobblestones.*

WHISPERS: Who killed cockatoo? Who killed / cockatoo?
ABIGAIL: *Mum! I'm coming! Please wait!*
> ABIGAIL *runs on, wildly, as the whispered chant gets louder ...*
> **'She dived into the first opening she noticed. Its uneven cobbles ran sluggishly with thick green slime.'**

WHISPERS: Who killed cockatoo? Who killed cockatoo?
> *The whisperers emerge from the darkness.* ABIGAIL *backs away in fear as they close in on her.*

ABIGAIL: What's that? What's that?
> ABIGAIL *is surrounded by The Push gang—***'wiry, hard-faced little fellows'** *who twitter ominously.* PUSHER 3 *is* **'a man on a little low trolley like a child's push-cart.'** *He leers up at her.*

PUSHER 1: Who killed Cockatoo?
PUSHER 2: I, said the Mawpawk, with my tomahawk:
I killed Cockatoo.

ACT ONE

PUSHER 1: Who caught her blood?
PUSHER 3: I, said the Lark, with this piece of bark:
I caught her blood.
PUSHER 1: Who'll be chief mourner?
PUSHER 4: I, said the Plover, for I was her lover:
I'll be chief mourner.
PUSHER 1: Who'll dig her grave?
PUSHER 5: I, said the Wombat, my nails for my spade:
I'll dig her grave.
PUSHER 1: Then droop'd every head,
And ceas'd every song,
As onward they sped,
All mournful along. All join in a ring,
With wing linking wing,
And trilling and twittering,
Around her grave sing:
PUSHERS: Who killed cockatoo? Who killed cockatoo? Who killed cockatoo?
ABIGAIL: *Mum! Beatie! Granny! Help!*

> KATHY, BEATIE *and* GRANNY *appear in the distance—conjured by* ABIGAIL*'s call.*
>
> *An enormous figure behind* ABIGAIL *raises a hessian bag high and places it over her head.*
>
> ABIGAIL *gives a bloodcurdling scream ...*

END OF ACT ONE

INTERVAL

SWEETHEARTS AND TREASURE MAPS FOR ALL ...

ACT TWO

SCENE ONE

In darkness, Abigail's scream echoes through The Rocks ... and becomes the song of the SPAEWIFE. *It is the same tune as Kathy's—only this time with words ...*

SPAEWIFE: **O, I wad like to ken—to the beggar-wife says I—**
How all things come to be whaur we find them when we try,
The lasses in their dresses an' the fishes in the sea.
It's gey an' easy spierin', says the spae-wife to me.

Lights up on GRANNY, *who looks out at us, accompanied by the sound of wind and waves.*

GRANNY: My seventh grandmother Osla was Elf-taken one night while watching sheep in Orkney. She disappeared to Elfland for a long, long while. No-one knows exactly what happened to her there, for she rarely spoke of it. But on her return, she was pregnant with wean. And with that wean came ... the Gift.

The SPAEWIFE*'s invisible voice sings again ...*

SPAEWIFE: **O, I wad like to ken—to the beggar-wife says I—**
Why lads are made to sell and lasses are to buy;
An' there's naebody for dacency but barely two or three
It's gey an' easy spierin', says the spae-wife to me.

GRANNY: This precious Gift can only be owned by a Spaewife. Now, a Spaewife can come from any land at any time, and she can go by many, many names, but where I come from, we use the word Spaewife. A Spaewife holds a secret power within her. She can hear voices that sing to her on the wind, across oceans of time. It is a power far more divine than that of any Wise Man, but the Spaewife is not a witch, for a witch deals only in *maleficium*. Yet the two are often confused for each other, and so the world has seen far too many Spaewives hanged, burned, stoned, drawn, quartered, and murdered for their Gift.

ACT TWO

SPAEWIFE: **O, I wad like to ken—to the beggar-wife says I—**
Why courage is shure to women as killin' is to kye,
Why God has filled the yearth sae fu' o' things for men.
It's gey an' easy spierin', says the spae-wife to me.

GRANNY: Ye see, witches can take the form of any living being … but only a woman can be a Spaewife.

The SPAEWIFE *appears, cloaked and masked.*

The Gift can be passed down by the men of a family, but never possessed by them. And it was my seventh grandmother Osla's child, fathered in Elfland, who brought the Gift to the mortal world. Brought it to our family.

The SPAEWIFE *sings on …*

SPAEWIFE: **O, I wad like to ken—to the beggar wife says I—**
The reason o' the cause an' the wherefore o' the why,
Why sae many of life's riddles brings the tear into my e'e.
It's gey an' easy spierin', says the spae-wife to me.

A wind curls and buffets their skirts. BEATIE *appears and watches fearfully.*

GRANNY: One day, as a wee bairn, as I stood on a cliff overlooking the Norwegian Sea, grass of Parnassus tickling my heels, the wind came to me and tole me of the Gift I held inside me. And that same wind also tole me of a Prophecy. A terrible but necessary Prophecy, to keep our Gift alive …

The SPAEWIFE *removes her cloak and reveals herself to be …* ABIGAIL. *She calls out.*

SPAEWIFE ABIGAIL: *Alice!*

SPAEWIFE ABIGAIL *starts to whisper softly, inaudibly, her eyes wide as she stares out at us.*

GRANNY: And then the wind whispered to me that one day I would meet the Stranger, and that they would be responsible for the survival of our line.

SPAEWIFE ABIGAIL *puts her hood back over her head and starts to walk away …*

I have been waiting for the Stranger for nearly sixty years now. And just when I finally have her … she disappears.

SPAEWIFE ABIGAIL *is gone from sight.*

I fear those wicked little elves have stolen another of our women.

And yet I also fear this Stranger Abigail Kirk may not be a Spaewife at all …

But a witch with a heart of *maleficium*.

BEATIE *covers her ears and runs away.* GRANNY *closes her eyes and raises her hands.*

As she calls on her Gift, she speaks / sings …

GRANNY: **O, I wad like to ken—to the spae-wife says I—**
The reason o' the cause an' the wherefore o' the why …
O, I wad like to ken—to the spae-wife says I—
The reason o' the cause an' the wherefore o' the why—
O, I wad like to ken—to the spae-wife says I …

SCENE TWO

Lights up on ABIGAIL, *her head bagged. She sits in a dark room shadowed with strange shapes. She clutches Johnny Whites' handkerchief in her bound hands.*

ABIGAIL: Help! Help me! Help—

The bag is ripped from her head. ABIGAIL *looks around with wild eyes. Before her* **'stood a mountainous woman with a hairy chin. There seemed no end to her in her full skirts and vast blouse of gaudy striped silk.'**

HANNAH: Near ripped me bleedin' beard out, yer did! I'll have yer bald, yer little bandicoot, see how you like it!

A man, dressed in **'well-fitted breeches and a tailored coat, and holding a tiny bouquet of jonquils and fern to his nose'** *appears.*

ERNEST: Hannah, darling, hold on now. We've caught ourselves quite the pretty little canary bird here. She'll go for a sweet sum—fifteen quid at least, methinks. But not if you take her tresses out at the roots. Ahahaha.

ABIGAIL *looks around, wide-eyed. There was no way she could fight her way out.*

ACT TWO

PUSHER 3: What do you reckon, Ernie? Proper bit of frock, isn't she?

ERNEST leaps in surprise to see PUSHER 3 *at his feet.*

ERNEST: Are you still here, Ralph?

He hands over a bag of coins.

Here's payment to The Push. Send my regards.

He kicks him away and turns back to ABIGAIL.

Out on a sojourn, are you, China doll? Ahahaha. Not to worry. Hannah will see you right. Heart of gold, Hannah, somewhere, amidst all of … that. And you like gold, don't you, ducky?

He removes her watch and reads the inscription.

'Margaret'. Is that your name? Doesn't suit you at all. Not to worry, we'll come up with something more fitting.

ABIGAIL *tries to scream again, muffled against the handkerchief.*

She's to be kept close. I don't want anyone laying eyes on her yet. I think she'll set off quite a little wage war. So no damaged goods, understand, Hannah?

HANNAH: I'll treat 'er like she was one of me own family, Master.

ERNEST: Oh, hurrah. Ahahaha. I'll be back in a sniff.

And he walks out, sniffing his jonquils.

HANNAH: Count your lucky eggs the master took a fancy to yer, duck, or ye'd be high-steppin' the cobblestones of Cumberland Place by now. Now get yourself flash or I'll 'ave to smack yer.

She walks away, leaving ABIGAIL *bound and gagged and wide-eyed with terror as she looks around the dark attic space.* **'A woman with tangled hay-like hair, cheeks bonfire red with either rouge or fever and a body hung with parti-coloured rags'** *stares back at her.* ABIGAIL *begs through her stuffed handkerchief for* DOLLY *to let her go.* DOLLY *walks over and removes the handkerchief from* ABIGAIL*'s mouth.*

ABIGAIL: *Help! Somebody help me! Please!*

But the ragged woman just stares back at her. Another woman saunters over. **'She was fancily dressed, with much flouncing and many ribbons, and a large hat with a purple ostrich feather.'**

MAUDE: Scream all yer like, duck. No-one will come for yer. Screams don't mean much on The Rocks. 'Specially if they come from a lady. They just get carried away on the wind, don't they, Doll?

> DOLLY *nods.* MAUDE *fingers* ABIGAIL's *cross necklace as* ABIGAIL's *eyes dart around the space.*

I'm the dress-lodger, Em'ly, by the way, but I call meself Maude 'cos it's more posh-like, don't ye reckon?

> ABIGAIL *just stares at* MAUDE. MAUDE *drags her closer by the necklace.*

I said don't ye reckon me name is posh-like?

> DOLLY *nods a warning to* ABIGAIL.

ABIGAIL: Yes. Very posh. Like.

MAUDE: This 'ere's a real ostrich fevva! Like an emu but more refined, y'know?

You know why I've got such a big fevva? Because I'm top bird 'ere, girly girl. In't I, Dolly?

> DOLLY *nods vehemently.*

So don't fink you can come in 'ere all curds and whey and pickpocket me fevva, Little Miss Muffet. I'm this close to payin' off me debt to Ernest and then I'm gonna set up me own establishment right in the middle of the goldfields. 'Maudellos'. It's Eye-talian—classy, hey? So you try gettin' ahead of me and I'll see to it that The Push aren't such gentlemens next time yer stumble down the Suez. Understand?

ABIGAIL: I understand.

MAUDE: Come on, Doll, the lamps is lit. Time we was hittin' the frog.

> DOLLY *begins to cough violently.*

Oy, Hannah! You can high-step wi' me tonight instead of Dolly. She'd scare off a rabid rat with that racket.

HANNAH: Bugger orf. I high-stepped from here to bloody Surry Hills last night. Bunions as big as onions. Look.

MAUDE: Come on, Hannah. I'll make it werf yer while. Tickle yer beard wiv me ostrich fevva.

> *She teases* HANNAH *with her feather. The big woman smiles. She cannot resist* MAUDE.

HANNAH: Orright then, ye little bloody tease.

> MAUDE *peers at* ABIGAIL*'s crucifix again.*

MAUDE: What a pretty necklace. But best get rid of him, ducky. Frightens off the clientele.

> MAUDE *pulls* ABIGAIL*'s cross from her neck.*

Welcome to The Rocks, Miss Magdalene.

> HANNAH *follows* MAUDE. DOLLY *reaches out to her aunt, her fingers grasping at air, grunting slightly.* **'Hannah stops and digs into a depthless pocket and fishes up a small bottle.'**

HANNAH: Here y'are, then, Dorothea. Don't say I ain't a good aunt to you.

> *She hands* DOLLY *the bottle.*

Bin 'ere since she was thirteen, she has. Her parents died in England and the parish sent out 'ere on the good ship *Corona*. I bin lookin' after 'er ever since.

MAUDE: *Hannah!* Move your 'airy arse before them Chinatown queens get me best fellas!

HANNAH: Plonk your judgement outside, duck. Some of us get put here. Some of us prefer it here. And some of us have nowhere else to go. Get 'er lookin' jammy, Dolly. The night's just beginnin'.

> HANNAH *kisses* DOLLY *tenderly on the head and leaves.* ABIGAIL *strains with her bound wrists as* DOLLY *drinks the gin.*

ABIGAIL: Dorothea? Is that your real name?

> DOLLY *nods.*

Where are we, Dorothea?

> DOLLY *gestures to the room.*

Yes, but where in Sydney are we?

> DOLLY *shrugs.*

You have to help me get out of here. How do I get out / of—

> DOLLY *suddenly starts to sing 'Comin' Thro' the Rye'. She has an utterly exquisite voice—one that stuns* ABIGAIL.

DOLLY: **O, my body's a' wet, poor body,**
My body's seldom dry:

> **They draggled up my petticoatie,**
> **Comin thro' the rye!**

ABIGAIL: [*spoken*] Dorothea, please—
DOLLY: **Comin thro' the rye, poor body,**
> **Comin thro' the rye,**
> **They draggled up my petticoatie,**
> **Comin thro' the rye!**

ABIGAIL realises she has been freed from her binds.

ABIGAIL: You untied me. Thank you, Dorothea.

DOLLY smiles. ABIGAIL hurries to a window.

We're above the Suez Canal, just off George Street. I can smell the Quay.

Music starts nearby. Loud drunken voices. Music. Squeals. Shouts.

Let's get out of here. We'll climb through the window and we'll crawl across the rooftops, past The Push.

DOLLY looks confused. She points to herself.

I'll take you with me, Dorothea. You don't want to stay here, do you?
ERNEST: [*offstage*] Ahaha!
ABIGAIL: Come on! Hurry!

ABIGAIL reaches out a hand to DOLLY. The girl goes to take it when in bursts ERNEST, HANNAH, and a MAN in a doctor's plague mask, cloak and top hat. He looks terrifying.

ERNEST: Keep her still, Hannah, so our guest can have good lookywooky.

HANNAH gets behind her and pins her arms. ABIGAIL screams and struggles against the woman's grip.

ABIGAIL: What? No. No! I won't do it! Please! No!
HANNAH: Ducky, this is gonna hurt me more than it hurts you!

ERNEST whispers to ABIGAIL.

ERNEST: He's a doctor, ducky. Lucky you.
CLOAKED MAN: How much is she?
ERNEST: Make me an offer.

He sniffs his bouquet coyly.

ACT TWO

CLOAKED MAN: Ten.

ERNEST: For this little innocent? Ahahaha. You do make me giggle, Doctor. She's gentle as a baby lamb. Isn't that right, Hannah?

> HANNAH *is still struggling with* ABIGAIL.

HANNAH: Aye. Baby ... lamb ...

CLOAKED MAN: Fifteen then.

ERNEST: Oh, hurrah! That's very generous of you. Ahahaha. But I have had several other offers tonight. Let me see what they think and we can take it from there.

CLOAKED MAN: I'll give you twenty.

ERNEST: Twenty? Oh, how lovely! Dolly here has never had more than ten offered her, isn't that right, Dolly?

> DOLLY *nods, wide-eyed and smiling.*

And yet this one's more than twice the catch of Dolly. So do I hear twenty-five, doctor?

> *The* CLOAKED MAN *stays silent.* ERNEST *gets in close to* ABIGAIL *and inhales.*

I'm quite taken with her myself, actually. So maybe I'll keep her an incy-wincy bit longer.

CLOAKED MAN: Fifty.

> *Everyone looks stunned.*

ERNEST: ... Fifty ...?

CLOAKED MAN: That's my final offer. Take it or leave it.

ERNEST: Sold to the lucky man in the fetching plague mask. Ahahaha.

> ERNEST *holds out a hand. The* CLOAKED MAN *hands him a bag.* ERNEST *opens it, beaming, then ...*

Wait. Are these ... chocolate coins?

> *He is suddenly floored by the* CLOAKED MAN, *who removes his mask to reveal he is* JUDAH!

ABIGAIL: Judah!

JUDAH: Stay back, Abby!

> *He tries to move her out of the way as members of The Push arrive.*

ABIGAIL: I've told you before, Judah, I can take care of myself!

> ABIGAIL *kicks a Push member to the ground and joins in the fight.*
>
> *She and* JUDAH *make a fine team as they fight off Push and brothel members, applauded by* DOLLY, *who joins in a little herself, as does* MAUDE.
>
> HANNAH *gets* JUDAH *in a headlock, but* ABIGAIL *saves the day, as well as stealing back her watch from* ERNEST. *He gives a final 'Ahaha' before she knocks him flat.*
>
> *It is a brutal, brash and brazen battle that involves garters, plague masks, ostrich feathers, jonquils and a smashed bottle of gin. But in the end,* ERNEST *and The Push are beaten.*
>
> BEATIE *is suddenly at the window. She unlocks it and opens it wide.*

BEATIE: Hurry, Judah. There's more Push on the way.

JUDAH: Is the ladder in place?

BEATIE: Aye. About five rooftops across.

JUDAH: Run ahead and keep an eye out.

BEATIE: Are ye alright, Abby?

ABIGAIL: Yes, Beatie.

BEATIE: Well, ye won't be when ye get home, ye peedie whelp, 'cos I'm gonna punch ye yeller and green!

> BEATIE *hurries away.*

JUDAH: Come on, Abigail. Let me help ye out.

> ABIGAIL *hesitates.*

Hurry now, Abby!

> *But instead,* ABIGAIL *turns to* DOLLY, *who is now holding the ostrich feather.*

ABIGAIL: Dorothea, come with me. I'll take care of you. I promise.

> ABIGAIL *holds her hand out to the girl ... who shakes her head sadly and finally speaks ...*

DOLLY: I'm afraid ... I am very much ... caught in the rye, Abigail.

> *She coughs. There is blood on her hand.* ABIGAIL *takes off her watch and gives it to* DOLLY.

ABIGAIL: Here—take this. It's a timekeeper.

She gives her the watch.

Goodbye, Dorothea.

DOLLY: Goodbye, my friend.

As the world shifts, we can hear DOLLY'*s sweet, sweet song ...*

Can a body hear a body
Screaming through the groans
Should a body have a body,
When the body's not his own?

As JUDAH, ABIGAIL *and* BEATIE *walk back through The Rocks,* JUDAH *puts his coat around* ABIGAIL *to warm her. She lets him.*

Comin thro' the rye, poor body,
Comin thro' the rye,
They draggled up my petticoatie,
Comin thro' the rye ...

SCENE THREE

At the Bows', GRANNY is pale in a bed. DOVEY is beside her. ABIGAIL, BEATIE and JUDAH appear.

ABIGAIL: Granny?

She runs to her.

JUDAH: Is she alright?

DOVEY: She'll rally. She had to go deep to find you, Abigail.

BEATIE: That's how we knew where ye were. Granny heard you screaming in her heart. She used the Gift to find ye.

DOVEY: She's exhausted. I thought we were going to lose the both of ye.

JUDAH: No fear o' that, ey Abby? Yer a game lass, no doubt. Ye shoulda seen her, Dovey! She fought like a boxer. Took on The Push. It were better than any sailor brawl, I tell ye! Wasn't it fun, Abby?

ABIGAIL: It was. Eventually.

DOVEY *gives a wan smile.*

DOVEY: Sounds like ye had quite the collie-shangles.

JUDAH: I've gotta get back to the shipyard. Return that stolen ladder.

ABIGAIL: I'm sorry for causing so much trouble, Judah. Thank you.

JUDAH: All's over now, Abby. Fret no more. I hope ye dream grand dreams tonight, as ye deserve, ye little wild hummingbird.

He whistles like a bird and leaves.

DOVEY: Wait, Judah. Ye hannae eaten. Let me get ye some neeps and tatties before you go.

She hurries after him. BEATIE *whispers ferociously to* ABIGAIL.

BEATIE: What came over you, you blanky rattlebrain, to go down the Suez Canal? Could you not see it's the abode of cut-throats and mongrels?

ABIGAIL: You tricked me! I thought you were casting a spell to send me home and instead you just let me go wandering off into 1873! I've been here too long now, Beatie! My mum will be flying to Norway any day now and I'm still stuck here with you lot.

BEATIE: Don't ye be whinin' about yer parents when I swore on my own mother's grave that I'd get ye back to yer home. I just used the wrong magic spell, is all! If I lose my granny because of you, I'll take ye back to Suez Canal and let them have ye fer free! There's nae worse curse than the killin' of a Spaewife.

ABIGAIL: That word again. 'Spaewife'. What does it mean?

DOVEY *enters and* BEATIE *closes her mouth shut.*

DOVEY: A Spaewife is a woman with the Gift. She has a little bit of elf inside her, and she can see past and present all at once, as clear as day. The Gift has never revealed itself in Beatie and myself. Granny is the only Spaewife left in this family who can call on its power.

BEATIE: Aye. The only one.

She casts a warning glance at ABIGAIL.

DOVEY: Nevertheless, Beatie, any children we have will be in the path of the Gift and all it brings.

ABIGAIL: But what do I have to do with it? The Gift?

DOVEY: I don't know fer sure. Only Granny can tell us.

BEATIE: [*exasperated*] Ugghh! It's this way—whenever the Gift looks like it's dying out, a Stranger comes to make the Gift strong again and keeps us connected to the magic of our past and our future. That's why those of us with the Gift see what we see, go where we go.

DOVEY: Beatie. How do you know such things?

ACT TWO 61

> BEATIE *realises she has once again said too much. She clamps her hand over her mouth.*

Do ye believe ye have the Gift, child?

> BEATIE *shakes her head, backing away slowly.*

BEATIE: No, I just ... I dreamed things, Dovey, but they were only dreams—not time flashes, like what Granny has. We all have dreams, don't we?

> *She moves away. Wanting an escape.*

DOVEY: What kind of dreams, Beatie?

> BEATIE *tries to get out again.* DOVEY *stops her.*

Beatie. What dreams have you dreamed, child?

> DOVEY *has never raised her voice before.*

BEATIE: Oh, Dovey ... When I had the fever ... I saw my ma's death comin' in a dream but I didnae tell. While she was still walkin' about and singin' and laughin' and workin' the sweet shop, I dreamed of her death so many times but I didnae tell. I didnae warn her. And then after she died, I thought fer sure the next dream I'd have would be seeing my *own* death. As punishment. But instead ... Instead I dreamed something very, very different.

I dreamed of my own hands. Mine, and yet they were not these filthy little scrap hands ye see now. They were a *woman's* hands. And yet somehow still mine. And there was *no ring* on them, those hands. And they were holding a big book with a leather cover. But it weren't the Bible. It felt like an even more powerful book than that. And then in my dream, I took off my pinafore ... and underneath I was dressed in a fine coat and smart suit! And when I woke, I thought maybe I winnae die like my ma after all. Maybe I'll somehow live! Survive! And I wanted so much to tell everyone, but I knew if I told them about my own future, then I'd also have to tell them about the sadness I saw coming too. The terrible, terrible sadness. And so I kept them all secret. My dreams.

> *Beat.*

But that's why I'm sure I dinnae have the Gift after all. I mean, look at me. I'm just a wee lass with filthy scrap hands who's learned nowt at the Ragged School but how to walk with a Bible on me heid. I'm just Beatie Bow from The Rocks. Why would my own dream show me such a lie?

GRANNY: Then you're not to die, my wee Beatie Bow!

ABIGAIL / BEATIE / DOVEY: [*together*] Granny!

DOVEY: Oh, Granny, I thought we'd / lost ye!

GRANNY: The Stranger comes to save the Gift. But the Gift also comes with a Prophecy. 'One to be barren and one to die.'

ABIGAIL: What does that mean?

GRANNY: Of those who could pass the Gift on in this family, there are now no more than four—Dovey, Judah, Gibbie and Beatie. And of those, it now seems Beatie is to be barren and so will not hand on the Gift, even if she had it.

ABIGAIL: Why is it Beatie that's barren? That's a terrible word, by the way.

BEATIE: I'm completely fine with it.

GRANNY: The ringless hand. She saw it herself in her dream. She will not wed so she will be childless.

ABIGAIL: She can still have kids and not marry.

BEATIE: I don't want any bairns.

ABIGAIL: She can still marry and not have kids.

BEATIE: I don't want a husband.

ABIGAIL: And even if she doesn't do either, you can't put it on her that Dovey, Judah or Gibbie will die.

DOVEY: We know it will be Gibbie that will be lost.

> DOVEY, BEATIE *and* GRANNY *cross themselves.*

He hasnae made headway with his fever and it's been seven months since he sickened.

GRANNY: Which means that the Gift will be passed on through Dovey or Judah. Or both.

> DOVEY *blushes, smiling.*

ABIGAIL: You can't be a Christian and believe in this stuff as well!

GRANNY: The Saints themselves were magic, were they not? St Catherine could read minds. St Clare defeated an army of men. St Christina got up and walked out of her own funeral. If that's not the work of a Spaewife, then I don't know what is.

Now, time for the truth to be told, when and where have ye come from, Stranger?

ACT TWO 63

A beat. BEATIE *gives* ABIGAIL *a wary glance but* ABIGAIL *finally caves in.*

ABIGAIL: The Rocks. Sydney. The year 2021.

DOVEY *and* GRANNY *gasp. So does* BEATIE … *a little off-cue.*

GRANNY: Well, that's a goodly journey you've made. You must be here to do something quite important.

ABIGAIL: [*growing desperate*] I'm not. I've never done anything important in my life. I'm just the weird girl in the old dress whose own parents want to move as far away from her as possible. I don't believe in magic. I don't have any powers.

I don't have any gifts.

GRANNY: Then how did you travel backwards through time to be here, Abigail?

ABIGAIL: [*pointing at* BEATIE] Through *her*! Tell them the truth, Beatie! It's not me with the Gift! It's Beatie Bow! Beatie doesn't just *see* the future. She *visits* it. She comes to my time all the time. She appears in the middle of parks and playgrounds out of nowhere! The 'little furry girl'! *She* brought *me* here. So if you want answers, ask *her* and let *me* go home.

GRANNY: Beatrice May Bow. Is this true? Have ye been hiding the Gift, child?

BEATIE: [*to* ABIGAIL] You *promised* me.

GRANNY: We still cannae let ye go, Abigail and ye willnae get anywhere without the talisman that first brought ye to us. The dress.

ABIGAIL: That dress wasn't magic. I found it in an op shop in Katoomba.

GRANNY: But the yoke is mine.

ABIGAIL: What? You mean the collar?

DOVEY: It's Granny's, but we haven't stitched it yet. And yet there it was around yer neck when ye arrived.

ABIGAIL: How do you know it's yours if you haven't even stitched it yet?

DOVEY: We've been planning it. Look.

She gets a piece of paper out of her pocket and shows ABIGAIL.

The grass of Parnassus is Granny's favourite. We were planning on stitching it into the lace.

GRANNY: And do you know what my name is, Abigail? Besides 'Granny', for indeed all women have a name of their own.

ABIGAIL: ... No ...

GRANNY: My name is Alice Tallisker.

ABIGAIL: A.T. Those are the initials between the flowers ...

GRANNY: That yoke is the object that brought us together, Abigail. Somewhere along the way, you chose to pick it up and stitch it to yer dress. Everything we do has a consequence somewhere in time. That is why you're here.

ABIGAIL: But you burnt my dress ... You burnt the yoke. How am I supposed to get home if you burned the one thing that connects us?

GRANNY: That's of no concern to me.

ABIGAIL: But if I don't get home by Sunday I won't have a home to go to!

GRANNY: Ye cannae leave until ye have ensured the Gift will be handed on. That is your purpose, Stranger. And yours, Beatie. Our family's survival depends on it.

ABIGAIL: But what about *my* family?

> DOVEY and GRANNY depart in silence.

Hey! What about my family?!

> They are gone. ABIGAIL turns to BEATIE, furious.

I believe it now. You *are* a witch, Beatie Bow. Of the worst kind.

> As BEATIE runs away, she drops her locket. ABIGAIL looks at it for a moment and then ... picks it up, places it in her own pocket and hurries away.

> Outside the house, BEATIE weeps.

BEATIE: I dinnae want the Gift. I dinnae know what to do with it.

> She calls out to the sky ...

What do I do with it, Ma?

> She searches her pockets for her mother's mirror.

Ma ... Ma?

> She cannot find her.

Where have ye gone? Please don't leave me again, Ma ...

SCENE FOUR

JOHNNY WHITES *sings softly, facing the east, sending his song—*
'Walama' ('Come Back').

JOHNNY WHITES: ***Ngaya na ngyinyi winina***
Ngaya wingara ngyinyi
Birung gurung ngaya but but
Birung gurung ngaya but but

Ngaya na ngyinyi winina
Ngaya wingara ngyinyi
Birung gurung ngaya but but
Birung gurung ngaya but but

Ngaya na ngyinyi winina
Ngaya wingara ngyinyi
Birung gurung ngaya but but
Birung gurung ngaya but but

The song draws ABIGAIL *through the house to her own window.*

She finds JOHNNY WHITES *sitting on his balcony, staring out across The Rocks.*

Still stuck on that dress, girl? The one you lost?
ABIGAIL: I didn't lose it. It was stolen. They stole it while I was asleep and then they threw it on the fire and they've been lying to me about it the whole time I've been here.

Beat.

Sorry. I didn't mean to interrupt your … Who is it that you sing to?
JOHNNY WHITES: That's between me and the wind.
ABIGAIL: Mr Bow told me your wife died. And your daughters went missing. Your sweethearts.
JOHNNY WHITES: Not missing. Taken. I know where they are. Over there, in Randwick. The Asylum for Destitute Children.
ABIGAIL: Can you get them out?
JOHNNY WHITES: No.
ABIGAIL: What are they like? Your girls.
JOHNNY WHITES: My girls … Like no-one else in time.

Silence.

My eldest girl loves to sing. She has a voice that can make the birds join in. Sometimes, when Tallowolodah sleeps for a moment, I can hear her voice on the wind. And my middle girl loves to tell stories. She can just make 'em up on the spot. Turn a peg into a person. A sheet into a sky. Her dad into a princess.

And my youngest girl, she likes to run. Barefoot and proud. Across hot sand and cold cobblestones. She can outrun anyone, that little *gilygan*. Almost.

Beat.

And ooh, they love their dresses, my daughters. Just like you, Abigail Kirk. They'd gussy up in their mothers' dresses and parade around in 'em like they were Mary Reiby herself. We had to burn them dresses, when my wife got poorly.

Beat.

There's a lot a father can learn from his daughter, if he lets her teach him.

Beat.

Oy. Where's my handkerchief?

ABIGAIL: I thought you gave it to me.

JOHNNY WHITES: I never said you could keep it.

JUDAH: Abby! Abby!

> JOHNNY *and* ABIGAIL *look down to see* JUDAH, *waving from below.*

ABIGAIL: Judah!

JUDAH: Are ye alright, lass? Tonight was quite a night.

ABIGAIL: I'm fine. Thanks.

JUDAH: Hello, Johnny!

JOHNNY WHITES: Hello, Judah.

> JUDAH *loiters awkwardly below.* JOHNNY *rolls his eyes.*

Goodnight, Abigail. Goodnight, Judah.

JUDAH: Oh, goodnight, Johnny!

> JOHNNY WHITES *departs.* ABIGAIL *calls down to* JUDAH.

ABIGAIL: Do you want to come up?

JUDAH: Oh no. I cannae enter a lady's room when she's in it alone. 'Tisn't proper.
ABIGAIL: Oh. Well, can you at least sit outside her window?
JUDAH: I don't see why not.

He shinnies up the side of the house, using a hanging meat hook to assist.

They stare at one another in the moonlight, from either side of the window pane.

ABIGAIL: Judah. Do you know that I'm 'the Stranger'? That I come from another time?
JUDAH: Of course I know. Look at ye. Ye had to come from a different time, be it the past or the future. Or Elfland.
ABIGAIL: You know there's no such thing as Elfland, Judah.
JUDAH: I don't see why there couldn't be an Elfland. I've seen places just as magical on my travels. Barefoot kings and queens of faraway islands. Mad toothless pirates. I've heard whales singing from deep below my boat, getting closer and closer before they burst out of the blue. I've taken on waves the size of mountains and seen shores so white that I can convince meself they're covered in Orkney frost. Sometimes I just lay on the deck and look up at the passing clouds to show me spectacles unlike any on earth. Elephants with wings. Me mam's face. Once I even saw you.

He smiles at her shyly.

ABIGAIL: I don't come from Elfland, Judah. Time has just taken me by mistake. And now I need to get home—by Sunday. Do you understand?
JUDAH: I do. But I also know the power of the Gift. Ye cannae fight it.
ABIGAIL: How do you know that?
JUDAH: Because I seen the Gift at work since I was in me mam's arms. She'd know things quicker than Solomon himself, she would. She'd know the very day I would return to dock, fair weather or foul, and she'd have plum duff in the pot waiting for me, hot and ready to eat. For I do love meself a bit of spotted dick, Abby.

ABIGAIL tries to contain her smile but she cannot. JUDAH *looks confused.*

What?

ABIGAIL laughs out loud. He gestures for her to be quiet.

Shh. What? What did I say? What? Spotted dick?

He joins in her laughter, confused.

Spotted dick? Spotted dick?

ABIGAIL: What's a spotted dick?!

JUDAH: A fruit pudding. What else would it be?

ABIGAIL roars with laughter. JUDAH tries to shush her. They both settle down finally.

I like it when you laugh.

ABIGAIL: Me too.

She smiles.

JUDAH: Are there boats in your own land?

ABIGAIL: There are. All kinds. Boats that carry sheep and wheat and plastic and gold. Boats with bowling alleys and buffet bars that haul thousands of people into Sydney Harbour down there, week after week. Boats that can travel unseen, underwater. We even have boats that take people to outer space.

JUDAH: Where's that?

ABIGAIL: Up there. The moon. A 'spaceship' flew to the moon and some men went for a walk up there. Amazing, huh?

JUDAH: Damned foolishness, I call it. Your pardon, Abby, but what good to man or beast is that bare lump of rock?

ABIGAIL: That lump of rock controls the tides. Where would you be without them?

JUDAH: True indeed, but no man has to go there to prove it. Not when what we have down here is so beautiful.

He smiles at her shyly.

I like that you know things.

ABIGAIL *smiles.*

ABIGAIL: Me too.

JUDAH: I've a mind to have my own ship one day. If those feather-capped dunces that stick flags in the ground can do it, then so can I. Find myself some sunken treasure. Bring it back here. I'll take my faither to a fine surgeon and have his trouble fixed. And I'll pay a clever tutor to give Beatie all the learning she needs. And I'll see that Gibbie gets the funeral he wants, whenever that happens to be. And I'll build Granny a room of her very own, so she doesn't have to share with Dovey. And I'll buy Dovey a fine silk dress and the softest of soap for her poor burned cheek.

Beat.

And I might give you a hummingbird. A live one. That ye can carry in yer hands. And every time it flutters you know I'll be thinkin' of ye.

They smile at one another.

Mornin' star will be up soon, Abby. I best get to Walsh Bay for the dawn trawl.

He stands.

Since yer so keen to be gettin' out and about, how about cockling on Sunday? I'll be settin' sail for Newcastle tomorrow, but I don't mind a day on the coves when I'm back. It's about time ye saw more of The Rocks and the Harbour is a lot safer than the Suez Canal.

ABIGAIL: Cockling? On Sunday?

A beat as she considers ... then smiles.

I'd like that.

JUDAH: Bonny.

He climbs down from the balcony ... then turns back.

Bonny!

He departs. Behind ABIGAIL, *a small figure enters through the shadows.*

GIBBIE: I nearly died tonight because of you.

ABIGAIL: Gibbie!

GIBBIE: Everyone was so wrapped up in finding you that I have been sorely and poorly neglected. No-one came to read me *Treasure Island*. My chamber pot is full to brimming! One more ablution and I'd have drowned in my own bed!

He hands her a pot. She ignores it.

ABIGAIL: Don't waste your theatrics on me, Gibbie.

GIBBIE: Theatre is the devil's work. You may as well buy a ticket to hellfire.

Why do you look so different from us?

ABIGAIL: Because you're all pale, shaved, disease-ridden, British weirdos.

GIBBIE: And you're a very strange woman. You may be beautiful, but underneath I know ye likely have eleven toes and huge warts and a pet newt and the power to curse people to their ultimate demise. You could be cursing me right now.

ABIGAIL: What an excellent idea. *'Parnassus!'*

> GIBBIE *gasps dramatically as she pretends to cast a spell.* ABIGAIL *smiles despite herself.*

Are you really sick, Gibbie?

GIBBIE: Of course I am.

> *He coughs feebly. Once.*

I'm awaitin' God's trumpeting call. Each day could be my last. Each hour. Each minute—

ABIGAIL: Back to bed with you, you bloody drama queen. Go on.

GIBBIE: A kiss for a wee dyin' bairn?

ABIGAIL: Absolutely not.

GIBBIE: A lullaby, then?

ABIGAIL: A lullaby? I … don't know any.

GIBBIE: 'Course ye do. What did yer ma sing to you when you were a babby?

ABIGAIL: What *did* my mum sing to me …

> ABIGAIL *thinks … then starts to sing softly, hesitantly, a Vietnamese lullaby, 'ầu ơ vì dầu'* …
>
> **Âu ở … dí dầu cầu dán đóng đinh … cầu tre lắp lẽo gập ghềnh khó đi …**
>
> KATHY *appears in the distance, unseen, until the song's end* …

I haven't thought of that in years.

GIBBIE: What does it mean?

ABIGAIL: It means the softest of songs can be heard through the wildest of storms.

> *She smiles sadly at* GIBBIE.

I'm sorry you lost your mum.
GIBBIE: I'll see her again soon.

He coughs. Once.

ABIGAIL: Goodnight, weirdo.
GIBBIE: Goodnight, witch.

As GIBBIE *leaves her room,* ABIGAIL *gets Beatie's locket out of her pocket and opens it.*

ABIGAIL: I'm sorry I stole you, Amelia. But I want my mum back too.

A song from outside ... 'Sailor, Lay Back'.

ABIGAIL *closes the pocket mirror as* JUDAH's *voice rings out jovially.*

JUDAH: **'Twas a cold an' dreary mornin' in December [December!]**
An' all of me money it was spent [all spent!]
Where it went to Lord I don't bloody remember [remember!]
So down to the shippin' post I went [off I went!]

SCENE FIVE

Early morning—the sun is rising over The Rocks. Below Abigail's window, along Argyle Street, SEAFOLK *haul on a rope.* SAILORS *from all walks of life. Among them is* JUDAH *... They share the song around them as they haul the rope toward the Quay.* JUDAH *sees* ABIGAIL *watching from above. He waves at her, beaming. She smiles back.*

SEAFOLK: **Sailor, lay back [sailor, lay back!]**
Take in yer slack [take in yer slack!]
Take a turn around the capstan—heave a pawl [heave a pawl!]
'Bout ship, stations, boys, now be handy [be handy!]
For we're bound for Sydney Town some yonder morn!

ABIGAIL *helps* JOHNNY WHITES *unfurl bright white sails from his laundry to the* SEAFOLK *on the street then gets caught up in the sailors' dance with* JUDAH.

JUDAH: **That day there wuz a great demand for sailors [aye aye]**
For the Colonies and for 'Frisco and for France [*bonjour!*]

> So I shipped aboard a Chinese junk in harbour [*ni hao!*]
> An' got legless flamin' drunk on my advance [ey up!]

Meanwhile ... BEATIE *sits on a street corner and pickpockets a book from a passing* SCHOOLBOY.

It's Latin. Her eyes widen as she starts to read.

SEAFOLK: **Paddy, lay back [Paddy, lay back]**
Take in yer slack [take in yer slack]
Take a turn around the capstan—heave a pawl [heave a pawl!]
'Bout ship, stations, boys, be handy [be handy]
For we're bound for Sydney Town some yonder morn!

JUDAH *takes over the song himself.* ABIGAIL *sings with him.* DOVEY *watches from afar.*

JUDAH: **There wuz Spaniards an' Dutchmen an' Rooshians [*na zdorovie!*]**
An' some fancy fellas jist across from France [ohh lala!]
An' most o' 'em couldn't speak a word o' English [all speak their native language]
But they all knew how to hit the deck and dance. [Whoo-hoo! / Knees up!]

SEAFOLK: **Sailor, lay back [sailor, lay back!]**
Take in yer slack [take in yer slack!]
Take a turn around the capstan—heave a pawl [heave a pawl!]
'Bout ship, stations, boys, be handy [be handy!]
For we're bound for Sydney Town some yonder morn!

JUDAH: **I wuz keepin' watch on deck one balmy evenin' [ahhh]**
When my eye caught someone stowin' on the sly [oh my!]
But before I could heave-ho the bastid over [toss him over!]
She removed her beard and made me change me mind. [ooh-ahh!]

GRANNY *is in the kitchen, cooking. She holds her head suddenly. She looks shaken.* BEATIE *passes the house, practising her Latin. As the* SAILORS *head away, she sees* ABIGAIL *dancing and singing with* JUDAH, *jubilantly ...*

ACT TWO

ABIGAIL / SEAFOLK: **Paddy, lay back [Paddy, lay back]**
Take in yer slack [take in yer slack]
Take a turn around the capstan—heave a pawl [heave a pawl!]

BEATIE *storms off furiously.*

'Bout ship, stations, boys, be handy [be handy]!
For we're bound for Sydney Town some yonder morn!

ABIGAIL *and* JUDAH *are left alone.*

JUDAH: Till Sunday, Abby.

They smile at one another before parting ways ...

SCENE SIX

ABIGAIL *is peeling potatoes, humming the sailors' song at the table as* BEATIE *charges in. She carries a book of Latin.*

BEATIE: *Et tu, Brute?*

ABIGAIL: What?

BEATIE: *Tot homines, quot sententiae.* 'So many men, so many options.'

ABIGAIL: Since when did you learn Latin?

BEATIE: Since Mr Mitchell left his bookshelf unlocked. You're stuck on him, inna that right?

ABIGAIL: What? Who?

BEATIE: Judah. That's why yer hangin' around longer than Moses in the desert. Ye've got eyes for me brother. Ye should be in Norland by now.

ABIGAIL: Norway. And ... Judah and I have just ... become friends.

BEATIE: Friends don't moon over each other the way you two do.

She impersonates them.

'Pass the salt, Judah ...' 'Let me show ye how to tie a sailor's knot, Abigail ...'

ABIGAIL: Shut up, Beatie. You're just a child. You don't understand.

BEATIE: He's promised!

ABIGAIL: Promised what?

BEATIE: He's *promised*! To *Dovey*!

ABIGAIL: What?!

BEATIE: He's betrothed to her. They're going to be married.
ABIGAIL: But ... they're cousins!
BEATIE: So? Don't cousins marry in your time?
ABIGAIL: No! Yuck!
BEATIE: Well, here and now they do. Judah and Dovey have been betrothed since they were bairns in Orkney. They're going to be married as soon as he's out of his time, so stop ye bloody moonin' and keep yer hands on *those* potatoes, not my brother's.
ABIGAIL: But I've never seen him kiss her or anything. Not even hold her hand.
BEATIE: Kissing and holding hands is not for Orkney folk. We keep our feelings to ourselves, not like wenches from your time.
ABIGAIL: God's pardon?
BEATIE: Oh, I seen ye plenty of times underneath that big bridge letting laddies lick yer eyebrow like ye were Mary Stuart herself.
ABIGAIL: I'm sixteen. I'm allowed to kiss whoever I like.
BEATIE: Keep that behaviour in your own time and stay away from my brother. He's promised Dovey a garnet in a band of gold!
ABIGAIL: But why her?
BEATIE: Because he owes her that. After what he did.
ABIGAIL: What did he do?
BEATIE: Never you mind. But she's been saving her wifely goods for years now. Her bridal chest is close to bursting.
ABIGAIL: Ugh, bridal chests! It was a bloody bridal chest that got me here in the first place.

> ABIGAIL *can't help herself—she kicks the bridal chest hard.*
> BEATIE *gapes at her, shocked.*

BEATIE: You don't kick a bridal chest, Abigail! It could spill all of Dovey's hope and glory!
ABIGAIL: I don't give a rat's arse about Dovey's bridal chest, Beatie. It's a stupid bloody tradition anyway. It'll all end up as junk in the end. Believe me. I've smelt it.
BEATIE: The Gift is takin' too bloomin' long wi' you. Ye better be here for somethin' special, or I'll be takin' it up with the elves.

> GRANNY *is there.*

GRANNY: Girls. Enough. Beatie, go and read to yer brother.
BEATIE: [*groaning*] Which book, Granny? Genesis, Exodus, Leviticus—

ACT TWO

GRANNY: *Treasure Island*. He seems to have taken a shine to Long John Silver.

BEATIE: Aye, Granny.

She scowls and raises a fist at ABIGAIL *as she leaves.*

Hoc est bellum. 'This means war.'

ABIGAIL *holds back furious tears.*

GRANNY: Are ye alright, Abigail?

ABIGAIL: What do you care?

GRANNY: I know you and I come from very different worlds. But some things are timeless. Some things we all share, no matter where we come from or who we are.

GRANNY *gently takes* ABIGAIL'*s face in her hands and looks into her eyes.*

Ah, there it is. So you're in love, Abigail.

ABIGAIL: I don't know. I've never felt love before. Except for Mum and ... Dad.

GRANNY: Well, love is quite the shapeshifter.

ABIGAIL: Ever since I met this person ... I feel like time has broken its own rules and curled around on itself and come to a stop, just for the two of us. Everything feels so simple but so powerful and so full of hope. Like I can see a future, even if it seems impossible.

GRANNY *keeps stroking her hair.*

You think I'm too young to know, don't you?

GRANNY: Abby, I was wed at fifteen—younger than you are now.

ABIGAIL: Did you love him?

GRANNY: Oh, I did. And he loved me. Time stopped for us too. The love we felt for each other was frail and precious and wild. And as soon as we had it, it was gone.

Look into my eyes.

'She took Abigail's chin in her hand and made the girl look steadfastly at her.'

A figure appears before them. It's the young SPAEWIFE *with the dark-brown braid almost to her waist. Her face is shrouded in blackness. She sings eerily as she stands on a cliff,* **'a sea far below, leaping, boiling, a marvellous blue-green.'**

SPAEWIFE: **O, I wad like to ken—to the beggar-wife says I— Gin death's as shure to women as killin' is to kye ...**
ABIGAIL: Who is she?
GRANNY: A girl, not much younger than you. Newly widowed.
SPAEWIFE: **Why God has filled the yearth sae fu' o' tasty things to pree.**
It's gey an' easy spierin', says the spae-wife to me.

The SPAEWIFE *holds out her arms and leans over the precipice, buffeted by a wild wind.*

ABIGAIL: I can feel her ... Granny ... she wants to jump.

ABIGAIL *moves away from* GRANNY *and toward the* SPAEWIFE.

SPAEWIFE: **It's gey an' easy spierin', says the spae-wife to me.**
ABIGAIL: She's going to jump off that cliff ...
SPAEWIFE: [*spoken*] Come back to me, my love! *Come home! Come home!*

She leans out, further and further until ABIGAIL *screams as we have seen her do before.*

ABIGAIL: *Alice!*

The SPAEWIFE *stops, jolted by the sound of her name.*

Step back!

The woman steps back, confused. The wind dies down.

SPAEWIFE: **It's gey an' easy spierin', says the spae-wife to me.**

The SPAEWIFE *steps away from the cliff, blows a kiss to the sea, then turns and departs.*

GRANNY: Abigail. Come back to me now, child.

ABIGAIL *comes to, weakened, dazed and terrified.*

ABIGAIL: Who was that?
GRANNY: My own self, Abigail. When I was eighteen and had lost my beloved—Bartle Tallisker. My first and only. Shipwrecked and lost forever to the Orkney seas. I was so close to jumping, Abigail. Throwing myself into the serpentine arms of the kelp. And then I heard a voice on the wind. A woman, calling across time. She called my name, just as you did—for it were you, even if you don't know

it. We Spaewives are always calling to each other across time. Reminding each other to keep going. Persist. Survive.

She smiles suddenly.

Aye, that was a good flash! Like a sky full of lightning, just like the old days!

ABIGAIL: You lost your husband?

GRANNY: Drowned off The Noup. Not even nineteen, and yet he knew love well, for it was all we had to give one another in abundance. The same way that you love Judah. The same way, I suspect, that he loves you.

ABIGAIL: He does? But what about Dovey?

GRANNY: If any one of you love truly, then you will also know how to live without your beloved, no matter how you lose them. To the tricks of time, to death, or to some other.

She smiles softly.

I heard the wind whispering tonight, Abigail. The Prophecy is rounding out. Tomorrow, time will finally tell.

GRANNY *gives* ABIGAIL *a kiss on the forehead.*

As she leaves, a shaking, sorrowful song floats through the house: 'I'll Hang My Harp' ...

MR BOW: **I'll hang my harp on a willow-tree,**
  I'll on to the wars again,
  My peaceful home has no charms for me,
  The battle-field no pain ...

ABIGAIL *follows the lament ...*

SCENE SEVEN

... and finds MR BOW *in the confectionary store, shaking uncontrollably.*

MR BOW: **The lady I love will soon be a bride,**
  With a diadem on her brow;
  Oh, why did she flatter my boyish pride?
  She's going to leave me now ...

JOHNNY WHITES *is beside* MR BOW, *a hand on his shoulder, guiding him gently.*

ABIGAIL: Johnny. What's going on?
JOHNNY WHITES: I found him wandering down Argyle Street.
ABIGAIL: Has he been drinking?
JOHNNY WHITES: He hasn't had a drop. He's been looking for you. Says he's got something to tell you.

MR BOW approaches ABIGAIL.

MR BOW: Abigail ... I may have had half my head shot out at Balaclava, but not every day needs to be a forgettin' day. That's what my Melia used to say.

He beams, shaking ...

Today is a rememberin' day! And one thing I do remember, Abigail ... Your dress wasn't burned.

ABIGAIL *stares at him, stunned.*

ABIGAIL: What?
MR BOW: Your dress is in this house. Hidden.
JOHNNY WHITES: Told you I didn't have it.
ABIGAIL: Where is it, Mr Bow?
MR BOW: That ... I can't remember.

He wanders away, singing as he goes ...

> **I'll laugh and I'll sing, though my heart may bleed.**
> **I'll walk in the festive train,**
> **And if I survive it, I'll mount my steed,**
> **And I'll off to the war again.**

JOHNNY WHITES: That bloody dress, hey? Must be important, that bundle of skirts.

He leaves. ABIGAIL *sings softly as she toys with the sweets.*

ABIGAIL: **O, I wad like to ken—to the beggar-wife says I**
    How all things come to be where we find them when we—
DOVEY: Helping yourself to the wares. Feather fingers.

ABIGAIL *gasps to find* DOVEY *is there.*

ABIGAIL: Sorry. I was just trying to help Uncle Samuel.
DOVEY: Seems yer everybody's sweetheart, Abigail. Yer gettin' before yerself. Just leave them be.

An awkward silence as DOVEY *moves the lollies away from* ABIGAIL.

It was Judah did this to me, you know.

ABIGAIL: Pardon?

DOVEY: When we were bairns. Bonfire night in the Orkneys. He knocked me into the fire, facefirst. It was an accident of course, but the fire didn't know any better. Burned me like a little witch, left me as scorched as the devil's hoof. That's why I stay inside, ye see.

ABIGAIL: Because you think you frighten people?

DOVEY: No. Because they frighten me.

ABIGAIL: Dovey. Everyone's got their differences—inside and out. That's what makes the world so … beautiful. You don't need to hide from it.

DOVEY: This house is my world, Abigail. And all who are in it are all I have and all I want. But you … you're a hummingbird. You can go wherever ye like. Be whatever ye like. So don't take away what little world I have.

She places ABIGAIL*'s hand on her cheek.*

Judah is burned into my very soul, Abigail. He belongs in my world, not yours.

ABIGAIL: I know my dress wasn't thrown on the fire, Dovey. Tell me where it is.

DOVEY: Tell me ye won't take him away from me.

SCENE EIGHT

ABIGAIL *hurries away from* DOVEY *as church bells peal. It's Sunday. West Gallery choral music rings out across The Rocks. 'Bright Morning Star'* …

VOICES: **Bright morning star a-rising**
Bright morning star a-rising

JUDAH *calls from outside.*

JUDAH: Abigail! Abby!

VOICES: **Bright morning star a-rising**
Day is a-breaking in my soul …

The Rocks is suddenly bustling. JUDAH *spots* ABIGAIL *from the street.*

JUDAH: It's Sunday! Cockling day! The morning star has risen on The Rocks! Let me take ye on a grand tour! Come now, follow me! Right this way!

ABIGAIL *beams and he takes her—and us—on a grand, gleeful tour of The Rocks.*

Up here, Abby!

They run up some steps.

This is Windmill Hill. You can see all of Sydney Town from up here.

Dawes Battery is that way, where the Queen's Regiment keep an eye out for anyone who turns up unexpectedly. They must have missed you.

He grins at her. A congregation exits the Garrison Church.

And there is the Garrison Church in which we pay our sober respects before we visit the Palisades, The Lord Nelson, the Hero of Waterloo, the Shipwright's Arms, the Whaler's Arms, the Black Dog, the Sailor's Return, the Hit or Miss, the Sheer Hulk, the Brown Bear, the Ship and Mermaid, the Cat and Fiddle, the Australian Hotel, the American Hotel, the Italian Hotel, the Orient Hotel, the Liverpool Arms, and the World Turned Upside Down, not that I ever visit such heathen establishments.

He winks at ABIGAIL *and she laughs.*

And right this way is where we set sail! The magnificent Millers Point!

He takes her hand and leads her down to Millers Point. To the very wharves we know today.

ABIGAIL *covers her nose and mouth.*

Excuse the smell. Millers Point is also where the boats dump any unwanted cargo.

ABIGAIL: It's so different to now. Then. Where I'm from.

JUDAH: One day I'm going to be Master and Commander of my own vessel and I'll call it something grand and beautiful, but for now, that one is mine. I won her in a fan-tan match from a sozzled sea-dog.

ACT TWO

She's not much to look at, but …

He pulls back a hessian cover from a small skip. A scream comes from inside.

BEATIE *pops up from the boat. She is holding a book of Algebra.*

Beatie! You little scamp. What are ye doin' in me boat?
BEATIE: Algebra! What are you two doin' down here?
JUDAH: I promised Abigail a day cockling.
BEATIE: Ye think ye can just walk around on the arm of me brother? I'm tellin' Granny.
JUDAH: Oh aye? Then I'll tell Granny yer sittin' in a dinghy down the whalin' wharf instead of attendin' Sunday School.
BEATIE: I cannae take another lesson at the Ragged School, Judah. My knees are weak with curtseying and I've got a Bible-shaped dent on me heid!
ABIGAIL: Why don't you come with us, Beatie? Not every day I get a private cruise on Sydney Harbour. Not even in my time.

BEATIE *thinks on it.*

BEATIE: Alright. Bonny.

As they get into the boat, JUDAH *takes* ABIGAIL*'s hand and smiles.*

JUDAH: Climb aboard, Abby! Always right foot first. For luck.

As JUDAH *prepares the oars,* BEATIE *whispers to* ABIGAIL.

BEATIE: Granny said I was to be civil to ye and I will. But if I smile at ye, 'tis only from the teeth outwards.
JUDAH: Ready? One, two, three …

SCENE NINE

JUDAH *rows the boat through the water as* ABIGAIL *looks around in wonder.*

'The Harbour was an inhabited place. Barges with rust-brown sails, busy little river ferries with smoke whuffing from tall stacks, fishing boats and pleasure boats with finned paddle-wheels, sixty-milers, colliers, towering-masted barquetines with sails tied in neat parcels—every type of vessel imaginable.'

ABIGAIL: The boats! The ships! Hundreds … thousands of ships!

BEATIE: What did you expect? Noah's bloomin' ark?

ABIGAIL: What are they carrying?

BEATIE: Coal from Newcastle, cedar from the northern rivers, whale oil from Eden and wool from … sheep. I've been studying Geography as well, can ye tell?

JUDAH: And people. People from all walks of life, coming and going. Rich and poor. Hope-struck and hope-stricken. The free and the condemned. That's Sydney Harbour.

ABIGAIL: I never thought it could look like this … No Bridge to look up at. Luna Park is a just few cottages. Taronga Zoo is a forest. Kirribilli House is … Kirribilli House. Bennelong Point is a farm?

JUDAH: Those are oyster middens left by the First People. Now it's used for stock. Not goin' so well. I don't think cows are supposed to graze on molluscs. Here we are! Drop anchor!

They reach shore. BEATIE *leaps out excitedly.*

BEATIE: We got the whole place to ourselves! Them cockles will be shakin' in their shells!

JUDAH *hands her a bucket.*

JUDAH: Tuck your skirts up, Beatie! I dunna want ye drippin' all over me on the way home.

She does, then runs on.

Have ye ever cockled before, Abby?

ABIGAIL: No.

She tucks her own skirts up. JUDAH *averts his eyes.*

JUDAH: Sometimes the cockle will leave a wee track of itself in the sand. Look for that. Then look for the breathing hole. See? And then you dig.

He digs up a cockle and shows it to her.

Oh … she's a beauty.

Later, when we heat it up, this cockle will open wide like a butterfly. But the two shells always hold onto one another, no matter how hot the fire.

Isn't it a marvel? Have a go.

ACT TWO

ABIGAIL: I think I'd rather leave them where they are.

He smiles. They sit together and take in the view.

JUDAH: What is it like? This place. In your time.

ABIGAIL: Where do I even start ?... Walsh Bay there—all that rotten rope and rusted iron and dumped cargo—in my time, those are finger wharves where people come from all over to play and sing and dance and tell stories.

And over the water there, where you've got gum trees and campfires, in my time we've got tigers and elephants and giraffes with the best view in Sydney.

JUDAH: [*laughing*] No!

ABIGAIL: But some things haven't changed. When I come from, The Rocks is still a jumble of voices and languages and sights and smells. People still flock to The Rocks, they still work there and get drunk there and dance and sing and fight and sleep there ... But none of us live in The Rocks. None of us even live *on* The Rocks. We all arrived here, somehow, and The Rocks has taken us in, taken us on, despite everything. Even when most of us have no right to it. Even while we're still working out who we are. Who we could be. Who we *should* be. What stories we'll leave echoing across time.

Beat. She gazes around the sky, around Sydney.

Take *my* time away and there's this—wool stores and tea houses and cobblestones and rat traps.

Take *this* time away, and there's invaders and convicts and massacres and shackles.

Take *that* time away and there's oyster middens and ancient language and the world's very first footprints.

And right across all that time there's still this glittering water. That big sky. Those blue mountains.

Ancient. Timeless. Eternal. I hope.

Beat.

Judah ... how did it get so late so soon when all I want to do is just sit here a bit longer?

JUDAH *stares back at her wide-eyed. Then ... she kisses him. He hesitates, then returns it.*

JUDAH: Oh, Abby. It were wrong for me to kiss you in such a way. I'm sorry.
ABIGAIL: I love you.
JUDAH: God's pardon?
ABIGAIL: And I know about Dovey. That you feel like you need to marry her because of the accident with the fire. But ... maybe *that's* why I'm here. Maybe it's nothing to do with any Prophecy or Gift. Maybe time has broken all of its laws simply because Judah Bow and Abigail Kirk were always supposed to be together. Maybe.
JUDAH: Maybe.

> JUDAH *kisses her again. Deep and passionate, on the sand of a Sydney cove ... until ...*
>
> *A bucket of water lands all over them. It's* BEATIE.

BEATIE: Ye filthy harlots! I'll punch yer both yeller and green!
JUDAH: Cocklin's over. Get in the dory.
BEATIE: I'm not goin' anywhere wi' you two dirty bunters! How do I know ye won't row me straight to hell wi' yer sinful ways?!

> JUDAH *picks* BEATIE *up and she screams blue murder. They pile into the boat and start rowing.* BEATIE *admonishes them all the way.*

That ye could be such a Jezebel, slinging slobber with my own brother! Poor Dovey's expecting to be wed by January, with her bridal chest full and her ring chosen and the down payment made and yer rollin' around the cockles with this hedge-creepin' dolly-mop! We should have left you in the Suez Canal, Abigail Kirk, for it seems that's exactly where you belong. There's a word in Latin for wagtails like you but I'm too refined to say it. And dunna tell me it was a *brotherly* kiss for I were watching the whole time from amidst the pigface on the peninsula. Don't speak to me, either of you! I'm fair sick to the belly with disgust. And we didn't even get any *cockles*!

> *They have landed back at Walsh Bay.*

JUDAH: I have to tie off the dory. Go on without me.
ABIGAIL: I'll stay and help.
JUDAH: No, Abigail. I'd prefer to be alone. Go home with Beatie.
BEATIE: I'm not walkin' alongside a scarlet woman!

ACT TWO

JUDAH: Harken now, Beatie. No more of this nonsense. It meant nothin', ye hear? Go on now, off with the pair of you.

He walks away, leaving ABIGAIL *and* BEATIE *alone on the beach.* BEATIE *turns to* ABIGAIL.

BEATIE: Ye've done nothin' but no good since ye arrived here, Abigail Kirk. Things we held tight to just seem to disappear from our very hands when ye're around. Ye're as confounding as a sixth finger and just as bloomin' suspicious. I'm gonna tell Dovey what I saw and Granny will use her power to send ye back today, Prophecy or no'. And good riddance, I say, ye pythoness. Hssssssss …

ABIGAIL: Beatie. Please don't say anything. I know it's weird but I don't think I'm ready to go back just—

She stops suddenly and looks over BEATIE'*s shoulder.*

Where's that smoke coming from?

BEATIE: Blimey, Abigail! It's the confectionary shop! Our house is on fire!

Smoke billows above The Rocks. MR BOW'*s voice rings out …*

MR BOW: *The Rooshins is coming! Charge the heathen devils!*

ABIGAIL *and* BEATIE *run for The Rocks.*

SCENE TEN

Rocks locals gather around the Bow shop and house. Flames and smoke flicker from the windows. **'Granny was beating at the blaze with a wet sack'** *as* BEATIE *and* ABIGAIL *arrive.*

BEATIE: Granny! What happened?
GRANNY: Yer faither had a drink hid somewhere. He tossed the rum bottle into the fireplace then took off that way, searching for Russians!
ABIGAIL: Where's Dovey?
GRANNY: Ran inside to get her bridal chest!
ABIGAIL: That bloody bridal chest—
GRANNY: Your *dress* is in the bridal chest, Abigail! That's why Dovey went to save it!
ABIGAIL: My dress?

She looks at the flames, helpless.

Wait, where's Gibbie?

GRANNY: We couldna get to him, Abigail. He'll be gone.

> ABIGAIL *watches in horror as the flames grow higher. Suddenly she grabs* GRANNY's *woollen shawl off her back and the wet sack then races into the house.*

Abby! No!

> ABIGAIL *is swallowed by flames and smoke.*
>
> *The onlookers watch on as the flames grow higher and higher and higher.*
>
> *Below her,* JOHNNY WHITES *stands with a few other locals. They all hold out a white sheet.*

JOHNNY WHITES: It's the Bow house, fellas! Hurry! Hurry! Unfurl these sheets now! Roll 'em out, roll 'em out!

> ABIGAIL *appears on the roof.*

ABIGAIL: Come to me, Dovey! I'll help you!

> DOVEY *appears, shaken and coughing.* ABIGAIL *covers her with the wet sack.*

GRANNY / BEATIE: [*together*] Dovey!
JOHNNY WHITES: Jump, Miss Tallisker! We'll catch you!

> DOVEY *looks around desperately and then jumps to safety. The crowd cheers.*
>
> ABIGAIL *helps* GIBBIE *through the window.*

ABIGAIL: Hurry, Gibbie! Come to me!
GRANNY / BEATIE: [*together*] Gibbie!
JOHNNY WHITES: Jump, little fella! We'll catch you! Jump!
GIBBIE: I'm not bloomin' jumpin'! It'll be the end of me!

> ABIGAIL *casts a 'spell' on him through the window ...*
>
> GIBBIE *leaps away from her in fear. He is caught safely. He shouts up to her.*

I wasn't ready! You could have killed me, witch!

> ABIGAIL *climbs out onto the roof. Her face and hands are black with soot. She reaches through the window and retrieves the bridal chest which is charred.*

JOHNNY WHITES: Leave that behind, Abigail! Jump!

ABIGAIL: No! It's Dovey's bridal chest! Catch it, Johnny!

She throws it into the sheet.

ABIGAIL *looks around in fear as the house starts to crumble around her. She sees* JUDAH *arrive.*

Judah!

ABIGAIL *watches as he looks up at her ... and then runs to embrace* DOVEY.

JUDAH: Dovey.

JOHNNY WHITES: Jump, Abigail! Hurry!

ABIGAIL *stands on the edge of the roof. A voice rings out across time ...*

KATHY: **O, I wad like to ken—to the beggar-wife says I—**
How all things come to be where we find them when we try ...

ABIGAIL *stands on the precipice. She sees her mother across time and space.* ABIGAIL *joins the song ...*

ABIGAIL / KATHY / GRANNY / BEATIE: **The lasses in their dresses and the fishes in the sea ...**
It's gey an' easy spierin', says the spae-wife to me.

ABIGAIL *sings alone, smiling down at* GRANNY.

ABIGAIL: **I now see what I have come for, says the spae-wife to me ...**

ABIGAIL *jumps.*

SCENE ELEVEN

The ROCKS LOCALS *help rebuild the charred shop and home.*

MR BOW *is there, sober. They pat him on the back as he works.*

JUDAH *and* DOVEY *stand together, holding hands.*

GIBBIE *sits in a chair to one side, reading* Treasure Island.

JOHNNY WHITES *hangs out his washing high above The Rocks and looks down on them all.*

ABIGAIL *wears her green dress, at last.* GRANNY *smooths it, lovingly. She looks smaller. Frailer.*

GRANNY: Abigail, your work is done. You saved Dovey for Judah and now the Gift will have a chance of survival.

ABIGAIL: Will you be alright, Granny? The fire took so much from you. You look tired.

GRANNY touches ABIGAIL's yoke.

GRANNY: I'll have to live long enough to stitch this yoke of yours. So maybe I'll be around a wee while longer.

ABIGAIL: But what about the Prophecy? Does it stop now?

GRANNY: No. The Prophecy remains in our family, as it always has and always will. But without you slippin' through time to visit us, Stranger, the Gift would have been lost forever.

ABIGAIL: I don't want to be someone else's Prophecy, Granny.

GRANNY: You're not the Prophecy, Abigail. You're the Power. There's a difference.

BEATIE calls from afar.

BEATIE: What are ye dillydallying for? Do you think I want to feel my way home in the pitch of night, ye peedie whelp?

GRANNY: If ye need me, Abby, just call out. The wind will bring ye to me.

The rest of the family is there.

MR BOW: I'm sorry for all the trouble I caused ye, lass. Truly sorry.

He hands her a bag.

Some sweethearts for your travels. I've wrote your name on every one, so you may never forget who you are.

ABIGAIL: Thank you, Mr Bow.

She turns to DOVEY. They smile at one another.

Goodbye, Dovey. It's nice seeing you in the sunlight.

DOVEY: It's nice to be seen in the sunlight, Abby. Goodbye.

GIBBIE: You wrenched me from my sickbed, threw away my Bible, broke my window, and magicked me off the roof into what could've been certain death. I still have not forgiven ye, but I won't go to the grave with any grievance so I absolve you and you may now kiss my cheek.

She does, bemused.

ACT TWO 89

ABIGAIL: Goodbye, you little weirdo.
GIBBIE: Goodbye, witch.

> *She turns to see* JUDAH.

JUDAH: Goodbye, Abigail.
ABIGAIL: Goodbye, Judah.

> *They stand in silence for an awkward moment. Then ...* **'He kissed her cheek, a swift, brotherly jab.'** *She turns to face the whole community.*

Thank you. All of you. It's been … bonny.

> *A voice calls from afar.*

BEATIE: For the love of blanky heaven and all eternity will ye bloody well come!

> BEATIE *runs.* ABIGAIL *goes to chase her, but then ... she turns back and runs to* JOHNNY WHITES.

ABIGAIL: The handkerchief, Johnny.

> *She gets it from her pocket.*

I managed to save it from the fire, but it's pretty dirty. Do you still want it?
JOHNNY WHITES: 'Course I bloody do. It's mine.

> *He takes it.*

Where you off to anyway, *gilygan*?
ABIGAIL: Home.
JOHNNY WHITES: Ah. Lucky you, hey? *Yanu*, Abigail.
ABIGAIL: *Yanu*, Johnny. Thank you.

> ABIGAIL *turns away from her Rocks family and friends ... and chases* BEATIE BOW *once more.*
>
> *As night closes in, they run down mazy alleys, past carriages and stalls ...*
>
> *Running past the past until they reach the lamppost on Harrington Street ...*

SCENE TWELVE

The two girls stand face to face, out of breath, under the lamppost.

ABIGAIL: This is the place. It's time. Are you ready?
BEATIE: Ye shouldn't have kissed my brother, Abigail.
ABIGAIL: Oh my God, are you going to hold that over me forever?
BEATIE: How do I ken ye won't be back, worming yer way 'twixt my family? I saw the way Judah looked at you when he said goodbye.
ABIGAIL: Beatie, you don't know how powerful it can be. Love. Whether it's the way I love Judah, or the way he loves Dovey, or the way I love you … It's powerful. It's the most powerful thing in the world.
BEATIE: You love me?
ABIGAIL: I do. Very much. Do you love me?
BEATIE: No, it's not the Orkney way.

    ABIGAIL *smiles.*

ABIGAIL: However you feel about me, I want you to go to your headmaster and tell him all the amazing things you've learned all by yourself. Latin and Geography and Algebra and History. Tell him you want an education, girl or not.
BEATIE: I cannae afford such a thing.

    ABIGAIL *reaches into her pocket and hands* BEATIE *her twenty-dollar note.*

ABIGAIL: Give him this. Tell him it's from a faraway land of wealth and riches.

    They smile. BEATIE *looks at the money in her hand.*

BEATIE: Oh my stars! That's Mary Reiby. She used to live up the road!

    They smile at one another. Then … ABIGAIL *reaches into her pocket and hands* BEATIE *the locket.*

ABIGAIL: I stole your mirror. Your mum's lock of hair.
BEATIE: I know ye did.
ABIGAIL: You didn't say anything.
BEATIE: I knew ye needed her for a little while. And at the same time I didn't need her quite so much … because I had you. Ye thievin' peedie whelp.

ACT TWO

BEATIE *opens the pocket mirror and holds it in front of her and* ABIGAIL—*both of them reflected in it. Almost like a selfie.*

Promise me you'll remember me.
ABIGAIL: I could never forget the likes of you, Beatie Bow.
BEATIE: Honour bright?
ABIGAIL: Honour bright.

They embrace. Then stand under the lamplight. The Town Hall clock starts to blomm.

One ...

BEATIE: **Oh, Mudda, what's that? What's that?**
ABIGAIL: **Nothing at all ... The dog at the door.**

Two ...

BEATIE: **Oh, Mudda, what's that? What's that?**
ABIGAIL: **The wind in the chimney, that's all, that's all.**

Three ...

BEATIE: **Oh, Mudda, what's that? Can you see?**
ABIGAIL: **The cow in the byre ... The horse in the stall.**

Slowly, slowly ... the world starts to shift. The Rocks of 1873 starts to slide away ...

'The little oval of Beatie's face shone for a moment and was gone.'

The 2021 children's playground returns, with the children playing their game ...

VOICES: **Oh, Mudda, what's that in the shadows?**
CHILD: **A fox in its hole ... A hare in its burrow.**

Four ...

VOICES: **Oh, Mudda, I see something there!**
CHILD: **Close your eyes, bairn, shhh shhh, there there ...**

Five ...

VOICES: **Oh, Mudda, what's that up ahead?!**
CHILD: **It's Lynnie Lou! Back from the *dead*!**

Six ...

They all run, scattering. ABIGAIL *runs with them, calling desperately.*

ABIGAIL: Mum! *Mum!*

SCENE THIRTEEN

ABIGAIL *runs inside her apartment.*

KATHY: Abby? You're home!
ABIGAIL: Mum! You're still here!

She runs to her mother and embraces her.

KATHY: Hey, hey, hey … Are you alright? Where have you been?
ABIGAIL: I'm so sorry. For running out on you like that.
KATHY: It's alright, darling. I understand why you'd be so upset. It was a shock for you last night, finding out about me and Dad.
ABIGAIL: Last night? God's pardon?
KATHY: What?

She looks at her strangely. WEYLAND *appears sheepishly.*

ABIGAIL: Dad! Hi!
WEYLAND: Hello …?
KATHY: Are you okay, darling? You look … different.

She holds ABIGAIL*'s face in her hands.*

Sometimes I feel like you've grown up in the time it takes me to blink.

ABIGAIL *hurries to the window to look at the view.*

ABIGAIL: The Bridge is there! The Opera House. Luna Park! The Domain …
    Grandma.

MARGARET *has appeared. She is chuckling at something on her phone.*

MARGARET: Look at these otters holding hands!
ABIGAIL: Everything is exactly the same.
KATHY: Not quite. We've had a talk, me and Weyland.
    We both agreed it's all a bit silly, moving to the other side of the world. We know you probably need more time. We all need more time.

ACT TWO

WEYLAND: And I know I need to do better. I see you—so sure of who you are, so aware of the world around you—and I realise I can't take you away from all that. So I'll follow your lead if you let me. Abigail.

ABIGAIL beams and hugs them.

ABIGAIL: Thank you, Dad. Oh, I've got something for you.

She gives him the bag of sweethearts.

They're sweethearts.

Beat.

Actually, they might be out of date. [*To* KATHY] Now if you'll excuse me, I'm gonna get out of this dress. *Con yêu mẹ.*

KATHY: *Mẹ yêu con*, my little witch.

She embraces them both. MARGARET *stops her as* ABIGAIL *passes.*

MARGARET: Are you sure you haven't seen my watch, Abigail? I could've sworn I had it on here yesterday.

ABIGAIL: *Tempus fugit*, Margaret.

MARGARET: Huh?

ABIGAIL: 'Time flies.' Right when you least expect it.

She hugs her grandmother and leaves her looking very confused.

MARGARET: Oh, how lovely …

SCENE FOURTEEN

Back in her bedroom, ABIGAIL *is in her pyjamas, the dress beside her. She turns to her laptop.*

ABIGAIL: *Sydney Morning Herald*. Judah Bow. 1870s. Search.

She reads.

Nothing.

She smiles at the headlines.

'Duke of Edinburgh marries Russian Princess.'
'David Jones new shipment—finest velvets, ribbons, and ostrich plumes.'
'Bolting horse wreaks havoc on Pitt Street.'

'Ship *The Hummingbird* sinks with all hands.'

Her face falls. She reads aloud ...

'February 4th, 1874. Heavily laden with timber, *The Hummingbird* turned turtle in a gale and sunk off the coast one hundred miles north of Sydney. All hands onboard perished at sea.' No.

'Bright Morning Star' can be heard faintly. ABIGAIL *grabs the yoke and holds it tight as she calls across time.*

Granny! Granny!

GRANNY *appears in her own time ... She hears* ABIGAIL.

The 'one to die' in the Prophecy ... I think it could be Judah! Tell him not to get on the boat. Granny, tell him to stay away!

BEATIE *appears across time too. She has heard* ABIGAIL.

Beatie! Can you hear me?

KATHY *is there too. The four Spaewives look across time to one another.*

The Prophecy! It's for Judah!

ABIGAIL *reaches out for them and the crochet falls like rain from her hands. It was nothing more but two handfuls of crumbled threads. Nothing was left.*

GRANNY, BEATIE *and* KATHY *fade away, leaving* ABIGAIL *all alone.*

VOICES: **Day is a-breaking ...**
Day is a-breaking ...
Day is a-breaking ...
Bright morning star a-rising ...
Bright morning star a-rising ...
Bright morning star a-rising ...
Day is a-breaking ...

SCENE FIFTEEN

The sound of the tinny children's television show plays loudly.

JUSTIN CROWN *wades through his apartment as* ABIGAIL *helps tidy up around him.*

JUSTIN: I'm telling you, Francine, he will bite her again if she tries to touch his eye patch. There is nothing wrong with him, he's just decided he's a pirate for the time being. I know it's a bit strange to you, but it's what makes him feel safe and I have given him permission to go full Blackbeard if that little wench tries to take it off him again. Thank you, Francine. *Yanu.*
[*To* VINNIE] Come on, Vinnie. *Nanga.*

VINNIE: *Treasure Island?*

JUSTIN: Again? Sure ...

    VINNIE *hurries to his room excitedly.*

VINNIE: Yo ho ho and a bottle o' rum!

JUSTIN: Thanks for helping me clean up, darl. Trevor's back in Kalgoorlie and I completely forgot our nephew's coming round tonight. He's doing some research on our family tree. I can give you a twenty for your trouble.

ABIGAIL: No, Justin. It's fine. Put Vinnie to bed—I'll let your nephew in.

    JUSTIN *leaves.* ABIGAIL *hums the Spaewife song as she potters.*

JONAH: Uncle Trevor? Uncle Juzzy?

    ABIGAIL *stops in her tracks.*

ABIGAIL: Judah ...

    A figure stands before her. It's JUDAH. *Or the spitting image of him, at least.*

JONAH: No. Jonah.

    ABIGAIL'*s speechless. He smiles at her.*

And you are ...

ABIGAIL: Abigail.

    She stares at him wide-eyed. It's weird.

JONAH: Where's Uncle Trevor?

ABIGAIL: The Goldfields.

JONAH: And Uncle Justin?

ABIGAIL: Putting Vinnie to bed. Reading him *Treasure Island.*

JONAH: My favourite. Along with this one.

    He puts down a large book. ABIGAIL *reads the title and gasps.*

ABIGAIL: *The Life and Times of Beatrice May Bow*.

JONAH: Belonged to some great-great-great-aunt a while back. She used to be headmistress at Fort Street School. Thought the uncles could fill in the gaps.

ABIGAIL: *'Dux femina facti.'* A woman is the author of all achievement. Beatie! You did it!

JONAH: Are you alright?

ABIGAIL: Yes. I just like … history. Can I look at it? Do you mind?

JONAH: Not at all. Go for it.

ABIGAIL: She's even put in a family tree. Judah Bow. Born 1855. Died 1874 …

So you were the one to die …

JONAH: What?

ABIGAIL: Nothing.

She reads on.

Alice Tallisker. Born 1800. Died 1881.

She smiles sadly. Reads on.

Dorcas (Dovey) Bow—née Tallisker. Died 1881. Along with her daughter Judith.

JONAH: All three of them. The smallpox epidemic.

ABIGAIL: So Beatie was the one to be barren after all.

JONAH: Well, she didn't have any children, if that's what you mean. Too busy being a career woman. She left the breeding to our great-great-grandfather Gilbert.

ABIGAIL: Excuse me?

He points to the family tree.

JONAH: Look. Gilbert Samuel Bow. Born 1863. Died 1943. Fathered eight children.

ABIGAIL: *Eight?* That rotten little … I knew he wasn't sick. He lived till he was eighty, the little bloody fibber!

JONAH: I'm glad he did. I wouldn't be here otherwise.

He puts something else on the table.

I found this with the book. I think it's some kind of bird?

ABIGAIL: It's a hummingbird.

ABIGAIL *picks it up. She twitters softly and whispers a memory to herself ...*

They can fly backwards and forwards and backwards again in the wink of an eye.

JONAH *looks at her curiously.*

JONAH: Have we met before, Abigail?
ABIGAIL: No.
JONAH: Maybe in a past life.
ABIGAIL: Maybe.

JUSTIN *pops his head round the corner.*

JUSTIN: G'day, stranger! I've promised Vinnie one more chapter, Jonah. I've never seen him take to a book like this! It's amazing. You two want to order a pizza while you wait? The Australian is doing pick-ups.
JONAH: No worries, Uncle Juzzy. I'll go grab it.

He smiles at ABIGAIL.

Abigail ... do you wanna come for a wander through Tallawolodah?

ABIGAIL *puts down the hummingbird on top of Beatie's book.*

ABIGAIL: Yeah. That'd be bonny.

As ABIGAIL *and* JONAH *make their way out of the apartment and into Tallawoladah/The Rocks, they are overtaken by the thrum of Sydney—past and present.*

Resonating through it all are children's voices:

CHILDREN'S VOICES: **Oh, Mudda, what's that, what's that?**

As the children chant, BEATIE BOW *appears and watches* ABIGAIL *and* JONAH *walk side by side.*

She turns to us, just as she did when we first met her, her arm raising and reaching out as if to touch us. As the sounds of the shifting city of Sydney build like a symphony, BEATIE BOW *smiles ...*

And disappears.

THE END

SONG REFERENCES

'Oh Mudda' – From Ruth Park. Music by Clemmie Williams.

'Minnie o' Shirva's Cradle Song' (pp 24–25) – Traditional.

'Orra Bhonna Bhonnagan' (pp 29) – Traditional.

'The Rousay Lullaby' (pp 30–32) – Traditional.

'Mo Nighean Donn' (pp 37–38) – Traditional. Additional lyrics by playwright.

'Spaewife Song' (throughout) – From a poem by Robert Louis Stevenson in his collection *Underwoods*, 1887.

'Comin' Thro the Rye' (pp 55–56, 59) – From a poem by Robert Burns, 1782.

'Walama' (p 65) – Dharug music and lyrics written for the play by Matthew Doyle, 2021.

'ầu ơ vì dầu' (p 70) – Traditional Vietnamese. Lovingly shared from memory by Văn Thị Phương and Catherine Văn-Davies.

'Sailor Lay Back' (pp 71–73) – Traditional. Additional lyrics by playwright.

'I'll Hang My Harp' (pp 77–78) – Lyrics by Thomas Haynes Bayly, music by Wellington Guernsey, 1800s.

'Bright Morning Star' (pp 79, 94) – Traditional spiritual.

SPELL AND CHANT REFERENCES

Granny's spell (p 42) – From *Carmina Gadelica, Volume 1*, by Alexander Carmichael, 1900, with additions from playwright.

Beatie's spell (pp 47–48) – From a classified advertisement, Sydney, 1804, with additions from playwright.

Pushers' Chant (pp 48–49) – From *Who Killed Cockatoo?*, by W.A. Cawthorne, 1865.

www.ingramcontent.com/pod-product-compliance
Lightning Source LLC
Chambersburg PA
CBHW050016090426
42734CB00021B/3298